Series Editors
Neil Chakraborti
Department of Criminology
University of Leicester
Leicester, UK

Barbara Perry
Institute of Technology
University of Ontario
Oshawa, ON, Canada

This series builds on recent developments in the broad and interdisciplinary field of hate studies. Palgrave Hate Studies aims to bring together in one series the very best scholars who are conducting hate studies research around the world. Reflecting the range and depth of research and scholarship in this burgeoning area, the series welcomes contributions from established hate studies researchers who have helped to shape the field, as well as new scholars who are building on this tradition and breaking new ground within and outside the existing canon of hate studies research.

More information about this series at
http://www.springer.com/series/14695

Joanna Jamel

Transphobic Hate Crime

palgrave macmillan

Joanna Jamel
Department of Criminology and Sociology
Kingston University
London, UK

Palgrave Hate Studies
ISBN 978-3-319-86273-6 ISBN 978-3-319-57879-8 (eBook)
https://doi.org/10.1007/978-3-319-57879-8

Printed on acid-free paper

This Palgrave Macmillan imprint is published by Springer Nature
The registered company is Springer International Publishing AG
The registered company address is: Gewerbestrasse 11, 6330 Cham, Switzerland

Acknowledgements

This book is dedicated to my parents, to Mara, to Steve for his continued support, and to the survivors of transphobic hate crime. The aim is to raise awareness of the pervasive impact of transphobic hate crime on our communities, stimulate further research and facilitate access to advocacy and resources for trans and non-binary people affected by this crime.

Contents

About the Author

Dr. Joanna Jamel is a Senior Lecturer in Criminology at Kingston University, London, UK. She specialises in studying marginalised, under-researched and underserved groups to identify issues and facilitate the improvement of needs-directed services. She has conducted research on many aspects of adult male rape victimisation including: its representation in the print media; its incidence in male sex work and the specialist policing response to this crime. She has published internationally in these fields. More recently, she has also become interested in the discrimination experienced by trans people within the criminal justice system and has written about the impact of penal policies on incarcerated trans offenders.

Introduction

This is the first book to be dedicated solely to the discussion of transphobic hate crime with regard to the available literature. It examines this crime and the varying definitions, complexities and prevalence with particular reference to the Anglo-American context. This book also provides international examples where appropriate to contextualise the cultural diversity of trans and non-binary people and their experiences of social acceptance. It also addresses the negative social sanctions perpetrated for gender transgressions which constitute transphobic violence in its different forms. Furthermore, a more inclusive discussion of the phenomenon of transphobia is provided by examining the extent of social acceptance of transgender people within indigenous cultures. This provides a socio-historical gaze on the transgender experience in this regard as well as addressing criticisms within the literature of the 'Whiteness' of transgender research also discussed in this text.

The term 'transphobia' as applied here relates to the fear, dislike, hatred, rage or moral indignation expressed regarding individuals who are perceived to be transgender or do not conform to the socially constructed gender binary (male/female) (see also Transgender Equality Network Ireland (TENI), 2014). In this book, a holistic perspective is taken with regard to transphobic hate crime, whereby legislation, institutional discrimination, the victim–offender relationship, police and community responses are considered. The term 'transgender' is an umbrella term that encompasses transsexuals, transvestites, cross-dressers and gender non-conforming individuals. The popular abbreviated term 'trans' is also used to denote transgender at points throughout this book. Trans individuals' expressed or 'true' gender is incongruent with their sex defined gender. Their psychological need to recognise their 'correct' or 'true' gender is facilitated through clothing, accessories, cosmetics and/or body modification. The antonym of transgender is cisgender which refers to individuals whose current gender identity is consistent with their birth assigned gender identity (see Tate and Youssef 2014, for more information). This term is now widely used amongst academics, community members and organisations who are engaged in work with trans and non-binary people. However, it is suggested that by use of both transgender and cisgender yet another socially constructed binary has been created which is more divisive than cohesive. For example, the interpretation and application of the term 'cisgender' can vary according to its usage by in-groups (trans and non-binary community members) which can be derogatory in nature when used to emphasise the inherent privilege bestowed on the out-group (non-transgender individuals). Hence, I agree with Freeman (as cited in Brydum 2015) where he suggests that the term 'cisgender' recreates the gender binary, he also emphasises the divisiveness of this term and how it may be exacerbating divisions between transgender and non-transgender people. This debate with regard to the gender binary and the importance with which it is held is pivotal to the discussion of transphobic hate crime; the perpetration of which is often seen to be reinforcing the socially constructed binary and censuring those people who transgress female/male categories which are socially considered mutually exclusive.

What is also important in this discussion is the definition of 'queer' as described by Corber and Valocchi (2003) as naming or denoting identities and practices that '...foreground the instability inherent in the supposedly stable relationship between anatomical sex, gender and sexual desire' (p. 1). This terminology informs the research on this subject providing more fluidity in the understanding of non-binary genders and their accommodation both theoretically and practically within different cultures allowing more scope for people to present themselves in a manner which is aligned with how they subjectively experience their unique gender identity.

Currently, the attention being given to transphobic hate crime victimisation is gaining momentum. Trans people are a marginalised group within society, and until recently, their fight to get their needs, concerns and victimisation recognised within mainstream consciousness had been largely unsuccessful despite the determined activism of many renown international and national organisations within this field such as the Human Rights Campaign (HRC), American Civil Liberties Union (ACLU) and Gay London Police Monitoring Group (GALOP). That is, until the appearance of Caitlin Jenner (previously Bruce Jenner, Olympian) in 2015 who has garnered unprecedented media coverage for the trans community and the discrimination they face in a heterosexist and gender binary society. However, her approach is from her personal experience and can therefore lack a more comprehensive understanding of the multiplicity and complexity of discriminations experienced by trans people because of their class, ethnicity and/or sexuality. There has also been some criticisms of her conservative attitudes expressed in the *'I AM CAIT'* documentary/reality series, where she stated '*They [trans people] can make more not working with social programs than they actually can with an entry-level job,... You don't want people to get totally dependent on it. That's when they get in trouble...' Jenner added* (as cited in Hensley 2015). This was perceived as distancing herself from the trans community and criticising the work ethic of trans people. However, in Season 2, there is a more developed sense of self-awareness and increased willingness to learn from her more experienced social network of academics and activists, who accompany her on her journey to raise awareness of issues affecting the trans community. For example, the discriminatory legislation regarding the accessibility of public bathrooms for trans individuals was the subject of one of the episodes. The case of Gavin Grimm also highlights this concerning matter (see ACLU 2016a, for further details). Transgender adults' restricted usage of public restrooms under the discriminatory HB2 law in North Carolina on 22 July 2016 cost the State their opportunity to host the NBA All-Star

Game in Charlotte (Margolin 2016). The importance of this raising of awareness of the trans community and the issues affecting them should not be underestimated when considering the motivation behind transphobic hate crime which can be fear and ignorance discussed later on.

Research on the topic of transphobic hate crime and its incidence began emerging in the USA in 2001 (Lombardi et al. 2001; Xavier et al. 2005). However, in the European Union discrimination and inequality experienced by trans people were being highlighted (Whittle et al. 2007) by researchers and only later focused more on transphobic hate crime (see Turner et al. 2009). Also, a sea change in the concentration of research on this topic occurred in England around this period (see Kelley 2009), and more recently (Antjoule 2013, 2016) focusing on prevalence and crime type (Chakraborti and Garland 2015). Other research compared this type of hate crime with homophobic hate crime (Iganski and Levin 2015) and examined perceptions of the policing response, victims' needs and expectations of the police and reasons for poor reporting practice (Kelley 2009). The European Union Fundamental Rights Agency (FRA) conducted a survey of its 27 EU member States and Croatia in 2014 which found that in comparison with other members of the Lesbian Gay Bisexual Transgender (LGBT) group, trans people were the most likely to state they were attacked or threatened with violence and a third (34%) were physically or sexually attacked in the five years prior to the survey. Furthermore, a frequent issue with LGBT research is that references to the transgender community or 'T' are tokenistic or the results are often confounded by subsuming these varied groupings together (see Wolff and Cokely 2007).

It is evident here that irrespective of the geographical locale of trans communities, they are subject to varying degrees of marginalisation, societal and economic discrimination and violence. This book provides a holistic view of transphobic violence across international contexts and cultures, examining its prevalence, relevant legislation, the victim–offender relationship, policies and practice and recommendations on how to address this pervasive phenomenon. Provided below is an outline of the structure of this book which aims to enable the reader to negotiate the complexities of this under-researched type of hate crime that receives less political and press attention than those of ethnicity and religious-based hate crimes.

Chapter 1 provides a contextualisation of trans people's experiences of social acceptance and alternatively social disapproval (which can range in severity from verbal to physical to sexual violence or a combination of all of these in response to their perceived gender transgressions) within indigenous cultures. The reader is also introduced to the possibility of a 'third gender' and how trans people presenting with this gender identity co-exist within a community where the binary gender (male/female) still predominates. The remainder of this book focuses on trans people's experiences of transphobic hate crime from a principally Anglo-American perspective which is contrasted with European examples where appropriate to illustrate similarities as well as differences in this regard.

Chapter 2 critically examines transphobic hate crime and investigates the extent of verbal violence, psychological violence, physical and sexual violence within this context. Reference is made to key theoretical approaches such as socialisation and gender role theories which reinforce the normalisation of a gender dichotomous society. This discussion of the socially perceived mutually exclusive male and female gender categories will contextualise the discourse about offenders' motivations and justifications in addressing transgressions of gender normative boundaries in Chap. 4. The intersectionality of victims and their diverse identities will also be considered in relation to whether they identify as trans, male, female or gender-nonconforming and their ethnic and sexual identities which can exacerbate the impact of their criminal victimisation.

Chapter 3 considers the historically gendered nature of legislation which serves to reinforce heteronormativity and the gender binary nature of society will also be examined. Heteronormativity according to Berlant and Warner (2003) '…is more than ideology, or prejudice, or phobia against gays and lesbians; it is produced in almost every aspect of the forms and arrangements of social life: nationality, the state, and the law; commerce; medicine; and education; as well as in the conventions and affects of narrativity, romance and other protected spaces of culture' (p. 173). This chapter encourages the reader to challenge their conceptions of the perceived neutrality of the law and its regulation of crime. Furthermore, it will provide a comprehensive overview of the evolution of the law in England over time addressing the inherent inequalities and discriminatory aspects of legislation and the efforts made to protect trans people and recognise their rights. For example, Schedule 21 of the Criminal Justice Act 2003 amended by s.65(9) of the Legal Aid, Sentencing and Punishment of Offenders Act 2012 which made 'transgender' a protected characteristic to enable enhanced sentencing of aggravated crimes motivated by hostility against trans individuals. In addition, The Gender Recognition Act (GRA) 2004 will also be discussed in relation to criticisms of its pathologisation of transgenderism condoning violence against the transgender body through gender confirmation surgery in order to conform to gender binary norms. The Equality Act 2010 will also be outlined in relation to changes targeting discrimination against trans people and the increasing recognition of their needs and rights in society. International comparisons will also be discussed where appropriate regarding the protection trans people receive from gender bias crimes. Other territories will also be discussed to further contextualise the legal context in countries such as Ireland, Northern Ireland, Scotland, Europe and the USA.

Chapter 4 investigates the victim–offender relationship and the conflicting findings as to whether victims are known to their offenders or are strangers being randomly targeted because of their perceived gender identity. Offenders' motivations are examined with regard to their wish to punish the victim for transgressing the gender boundaries, or in some cases as retribution for perceived 'gender deception'. Case studies of Brandon Teena, Gwen Araujo, Chrissie Azzopardi and Destiny Lauren, for example, are discussed to illustrate the excessive violence perpetrated as well as returning to the earlier theme of intersectionality and its exacerbation of criminal victimisation. The pervasiveness of the direct and indirect victimisation will also be considered in relation to the individual, the community and the notion of 'safe' and 'gendered spaces' and how these are negotiated in daily activities. Thus, the potential negative and pervasive impact of transphobic victimisation on victims and their lifestyles will be illustrated.

In Chapter 5, responses to transphobic hate crime are critically considered and contextualise the recommendations made in relation to gaps in provisions in Chap. 6. In this penultimate chapter, the response to a transphobic hate crime by charities, policy-makers, criminal justice agencies and specialist police officers such as Lesbian Gay Bisexual and Transgender Liaison Officers (LGBT LOs) will be examined. Limited resources are available to charities and police, and hence a needs-directed approach is taken, thus the problem of extensive underreporting of transphobic hate crime is a cause for concern. It has been suggested by research that factors such as the lack of confidence in criminal justice agencies both in England and Wales and in the USA negatively impact on reporting practices. This will be discussed in conjunction with the methods suggested to improve reporting practices, for example, third-party reporting and their effectiveness. This chapter will therefore inform the final chapter's recommendations on responses to transphobic hate crime and develop important recommendations regarding policy and practice.

Chapter 6 summarises the key messages of this book. It also provides short chapter outlines that assist revision and synthesis of the pivotal themes expressed. Theoretical contributions of the text are also outlined and the importance of applying theory to practice emphasised.

References

ACLU. (2016a). *G.G. V. Gloucester county school board.* Retrieved May 20, 2016, from https://www.aclu.org/cases/gg-v-gloucester-county-school-board.

Antjoule, N. (2013). *The hate crime report: Homophobia, biphobia and transphobia in London*. London: GALOP.

Antjoule, N. (2016). *The hate crime report: Homophobia, biphobia and transphobia in the UK.* Retrieved from http://www.galop.org.uk/wp-content/uploads/2016/10/The-Hate-Crime-Report-2016.pdf.

Berlant, L., & Warner, M. (2003). Sex in public. In R. J. Corber & S. Valocchi (Eds.), *Queer studies: An interdisciplinary reader* (pp. 170–183). Oxford: Blackwell.

Brydum, S. (2015, July 31). The true meaning of the word 'Cisgender': It's not complicated: Cisgender is the opposite of transgender. *The Advocate*. Retrieved from https://www.advocate.com/transgender/2015/07/31/true-meaning-word-cisgender.

Chakraborti, N., & Garland, J. (2015). *Hate crime: Impact, causes and responses* (2nd ed.). London: Sage.

Corber, R. J., & Valocchi, S. (2003). *Queer studies: An interdisciplinary reader.* Oxford: Blackwell.

Hensley, N. (2015). *Caitlyn Jenner's conservative beliefs voiced on 'I Am Cait' may jeopardize her role as transgender icon: Activists. Daily News.* Retrieved March 31, 2016, from http://www.nydailynews.com/news/national/trans-activist-critical-caitlyn-jenner-gop-views-article-1.2311763.

Iganski, P., & Levin, J. (2015). *Hate crime: A global perspective.* New York: Routledge.

Kelley, P. (2009). *Filling in the blanks: Hate crime in London.* Retrieved from London.

Lombardi, E. L., Wilchins, R. A., Priesing, D., & Malouf, D. (2001). Gender violence: Transgender experiences with violence and discrimination. *Journal of Homosexuality, 42*(1), 89–101.

Margolin, E. (2016). *NBA pulls all-star game out of Charlotte over transgender bathroom Law HB2.* Retrieved from http://www.nbcnews.com/feature/nbc-out/nba-pulls-all-star-game-out-charlotte-over-hb2-n614466.

Tate, C. C., & Youssef, C. P. (2014). Integrating the study of transgender spectrum and cisgender experiences of self-categorization from a personality perspective. *Review of General Psychology, 18*(4), 302–312.

Transgender Equality Network Ireland (TENI) (2014). *STAD: Stop transphobia and discrimination report.* Ireland. Retrieved from www.teni.ie.

Turner, L., Whittle, S., & Combs, R. (2009). *Transphobic hate crime in the EU.* Retrieved February 15, 2016, from http://www.ilgaeurope.org/sites/default/files/transphobic_hate_crime_in_the_european_union_0.pdf.

Whittle, S., Turner, L., & Al-Alami, M. (2007). *Engendered penalties: Transgender and transsexual people's experiences of inequality and discrimination.* London: The Equalities Review.

Wolff, K. B., & Cokely, C. L. (2007). "To protect and serve?" An exploration of police conduct in relation to the gay, lesbian, bisexual, and transgender community. *Sexuality & Culture, 11*, 1–23.

Xavier, J. M., Bobbin, M., Singer, B., & Budd, E. (2005). A needs assessment of trangendered people of color living in Washington, DC. *International Journal of Transgenderism, 8*(2/3), 31–48.

1

Trans People and Their Experiences of Transphobia in Indigenous Cultures

Abstract Hate crimes recorded by and reported to the police are as diverse as the trans people affected by them. In addition, transphobic hate crime research favours an Anglo-American focus ignoring this type of crime in non-Western societies and their differential acceptance of trans people. This neglect of indigenous cultures is addressed here and the notion of a homogeneous transgender community is deconstructed. Lessons may be learned from these societies in order to be more gender flexible and accepting of non-binary gender identities. However, some First Nation Native American tribes and the Samoan community accept transgender or third gender people, but on closer examination of anthropologists' accounts (Lang 1998; Nanda 1990) this is superficial, as violence is sanctioned against those who transgress binary gender identities within traditional community life.

Keywords Transphobia · Gender flexible · Indigenous · Non-binary Violence · Colonisation · First Nation

J. Jamel, *Transphobic Hate Crime*, Palgrave Hate Studies,
https://doi.org/10.1007/978-3-319-57879-8_1

In the following section, the reader will be introduced to a varied group of transgender communities from a global perspective. This aspect is considered in order to raise awareness of the gender and ethnic diversity of trans people which is not often reflected in the available literature. Furthermore, the essentialist view which pervades research on transgender issues reinforces the 'Interplanetary Theory of Gender' that assumes women engage in a gendered behaviour via their biology or socialisation, whereby women will act like women and men like men irrespective of geographical location (Kimmel 2008). This essentialist view is challenged by discussing the gender identities and gender performances of the *xaniths* of Oman, the *hijras* of India, the *fa'afāfine* of Samoa, the *fakaleīti of Tonga,* the *māhū of Tahiti,* the *sistergirls* of Aboriginal Australia and the *alyha, hwame, winkte and lhamana* of the First Nation Native Americans, for example. Wherever information was available, it was then used to highlight the varying types of transphobic abuse experienced by some of these trans people which was socially sanctioned within their respective societies.

The Xaniths of Oman

Xaniths are of Omani origin and are considered to exhibit a distinct 'third gender' identity but are equated with women. Wikan's (1982) anthropological research focuses on the *xaniths* of Sohar, in northern Oman. *Xaniths* wear distinctive pastel coloured clothes combining male and female styles in their mode of dress and hairstyle. If legally permitted, they would dress as women, but this is banned and there are severe negative sanctions which are imposed such as flogging or imprisonment if they transgress this rule. The reason not being due to their male anatomy but because they are socially female and engage in prostitution, by dressing as women they would dishonour them, as female prostitutes are not considered to exist in their society. Nevertheless, *xaniths*' non-verbal behaviour is feminised, from their facial expressions, voice, laugh, mannerisms, and deportment. However, under Islamic Law they also possess all of the rights as a man, worship in the mosque with men and support themselves financially unlike females who are not financially independent. They also have male names and are referred to using male pronouns. Their varying occupations include homosexual prostitution (which is not due to economic necessity or 'survival sex'), as singers—which has a spiritual aspect at weddings, and they also work as domestic servants. There is a flexibility with regard to the *xanith's* identity, in that, they may assume the identity of a female for several years and later revert back to a male gender identity for the remainder of their life, he may then live as a *xanith* until old age or he may alternate between female and male gender identities throughout his life (Wikan 1982). This fluid gender identity of *xaniths* is permitted amongst males only. Females must retain their gender identity throughout life and hence an intermediate third gender role is inaccessible to them. *Xaniths* are neither men nor women so may again like the *hijras* be described as an alternate gender; however, they differ from the latter as they possess male and female characteristics and are not emasculated.

The Hijra of India

The term *'hijra'* (of Urdu origin) translated into English is 'eunuch' or 'intersex' (Nanda 1990). 'Emasculation is the dharm (religious obligation of the hijras, and it is this renunciation of male sexuality through the surgical removal of the organ of male sexuality that is at the heart of the definition of the *hijra* social identity' (Nanda 1990, p. 15). They identify with a female gender identity and role, but have masculine secondary sexual characteristics; however, some males undertake this role who do possess external male genitalia (and fear their discovery). The *hijra* also identifies with a predominantly homosexual orientation (see Kahn et al. 2009; Kalra 2012). *Hijras* self-identify as an 'alternative gender' by not identifying as a man or a woman. There are three modes of recruitment for males with genital abnormalities: (i) parents give them to the *hijras*; (ii) the *hijras* claim them; and (iii) on reaching adulthood, children with these deformities will join the *hijras* (Agrawal 1997; Nanda 1990). *Hijras'* explicit and '...exaggerated use of feminine cultural symbols in their self-presentation through their mode of dress, hairstyle, names and kinship terms was in considerable dissonance with their apparent bodily status which was clearly not biologically female' (according to Nanda, p. 287).

The primary role of the *hijras* is their performance at the birth of a male child or wedding ceremony to bless them and bestow fertility. Although *hijras* also engage in sex work when they are unable to find other job opportunities, some may be self-employed or work for non-governmental organisations (UNDP 2010). Monro (2010) differentiates between the *hijras* who have been castrated and the *Kothis* (who have not) but who self-identify as female and are homosexual. '*Hijras* are *akwas* (not castrated) and *nirvana* (castrated)—some *hijras* are *akwas*, so biologically they are men—they are also predominantly homosexual though they may be married with kids, but this is due to convenience, they are not bisexual. *Kothis*, are a heterogeneous group, who may exhibit bisexual behavior and marry women; they are of a lower socioeconomic status, and may engage in "survival sex" work. Some hijra-identified people may also identify themselves as *"kothis"*. But not all *kothis* identify as transgender or *hijras* (UNDP 2010).

Regional variations of other transgender identities include the Kinnars (Delhi) and Aravanis *Hijras* (Aravanis) in Tamil Nadu, where the Aravanigal Welfare Board defines them as biological males who self-identify as a woman trapped in a male's body (UNDP 2010). Jogtas or Jopgappas are devoted to and serve the Goddess Renukha Devi (Yellamma) in temples in Maharashtra and Karnataka. "Jogta" and "Jogti" refer to the respective male and female servants of that Goddess. To become a "Jogta" (or Jogti) it must be a family tradition or they may identify a "Guru" (or "Pujari") who will receive them as a "Chela" or "Shishya" (disciple). The term "Jogti *Hijras*" may be used to denote trans females who are devotees/servants of the Goddess Renukha Devi and part of the *hijra* communities. Whereas "jogtas" are heterosexuals who may or may not dress in women's clothing when worshiping the Goddess. They are also differentiated from "jogtis" who are natal females dedicated to the Goddess. However, "jogti *hijras*" may self-identify as "jogti" (female pronoun) or *hijras*, and sometimes even as "jogtas" (UNDP 2010). Shiv-Shaktis are males considered to have a relationship with a Goddess and who identify as female. "They are inducted into the Shiv-Shakti community by senior gurus, who teach them the norms, customs and rituals to be observed. Shiv-Shaktis are married in a ceremony as the bride to a sword that represents male power or Shiva (deity)" (UNDP 2010, p. 13). Shiv-Shaktis may occasionally cross-dress and use female accessories. In the main, they are of a low "...socio-economic status and earn their living as astrologers, soothsayers and spiritual healers; some also seek alms" (UNDP 2010, p. 13). Next, there is a brief discussion of the socially sanctioned levels of violence experienced by the *hijra* when in public spaces.

The *hijra* inhabit an institutionalised role that has spiritual elements within Indian society (Kalra 2012) and whom are venerated when hired to bless newborn infants, and wedding grooms with fertility. However, they are also treated with a combination of ridicule and fear when walking around in public. *Hijras* may be referred to using the derisory term *'kaurika'* (an old penny with a hole in the middle which is obsolete, like an 'empty shell' which has no purpose) by small and adolescent boys (Nanda 1990). Although this verbal harassment is stated as being carried out by young boys, it could be speculated that they may also experience harassment from adult members of society especially when engaging in sex work as there is the double stigmatisation (i.e., being a sex worker and hijra) and the possible conflict experienced by clients. They may be internally conflicted as they hire *hijras* but despise their desire to have sex with them. Thus, this self-hatred of clients of the hijra may have parallels with that experienced by those who perpetrate transphobic violence directed at transgender sex workers described in research later in this book. Therefore, it seems there is a level of hypocrisy with regard to how these trans people are treated. Whereby, they may be subject to verbal violence and censure despite their socially ascribed role in the community, these double standards where violence is socially condoned against trans people are also evidenced in other cultures and indigenous communities discussed below.

Trans People in Mainland and Maritime South-East Asia and Brazil

The *'bakla'* in the Philippines is a derogatory term used to describe males whose behaviour deviates from male gender norms, they self-identify as homosexual and their sexual expression includes fetishism and transvestitism. Their self-presentations are as effeminate males, 'sissies' or they may be perceived as being fearful or shy (see Winter et al. 2007). These males are therefore subject to social condemnation through their labelling as *'bakla'* which is also a manner in which wider society is socially condemning their performance of gender role deviancy and attempting to reinforce the rigid gender role binary. In Thai, *'kathoey'* is an umbrella term in South-East Asia to capture all third gender categories, encompassing all alternative gender presentations and sexualities which deviate from the gender binary. However, in reality, *kathoey* seldom refers to those who are natally female irrespective of their gender identification. There are also regional variations, as in Bangkok, in the middle classes, kathoey only refers to Male-to-Female (MTF) transgender persons (Kang 2012). There are also variations in spelling in the Thai language such as 'Kra Thoey' which in the English language is translated into 'ladyboys' (Wetsiriyanan et al. 2016). In Bangkok, again double standards are present, whereby 'ladyboys' are socially accepted within society but are also stigmatised and it can be challenging for them to assimilate into mainstream society. In Brazil, there are the *'travestis'* who are transgender sex workers, they are homosexual men who cross-dress from an early age, identify their gender through female names, undergo feminisation surgery, undertake hormone therapy, and use silicone injections to achieve a physically feminine presentation such as pronounced hips, thighs and breasts. However, crucially they reject the notion that they want to be or wish to become female. Their gender is defined by their sexual practice not anatomy and thus they ascribe to a 'third gender'. Their boyfriends must be quite masculine and be the active sexual partner never the receptive one. Although this is a homosexual relationship, the attraction is based on difference in that the boyfriend must desire women and the *travesti* desire males (Kulick 1998). In his research, Kulick does not document violence experienced by *travestis* at the hands of their clients; however, they may sometimes be financially exploited by their boyfriends, although it is described as an accepted practice that *travestis* may knowingly allow to happen depending on their level of emotional attachment to their boyfriend. When *travestis* are murdered, the term used to describe these crimes are 'travesticides' (Berkins 2015 cited in Radi and Sardá-Chandiramani 2016), whereas a more diverse approach to addressing such crimes defines them as 'violence based on prejudice' (IACHR 2015 cited in

Radi and Sardá-Chandiramani 2016). These crimes are predominantly street-based, particularly within those areas which are quite isolated and are usually perpetrated at night. The level of transphobic violence that is inflicted on the bodies of *travestis* and trans women is evidenced by the explicit injuries and marks left illustrating the extent of brutality and extreme cruelty carried out by perpetrators. The perpetration of such violence demonstrates that the offender does not see *travestis* as human beings but objectifies them and imposes a death sentence for their non-conformity to the gender binary while also sending a threatening message to other *travestis* and trans communities. Research suggests that offenders frequently do not have any family connections to the victims; however, it was usually found to be members of police forces or persons with links to them (Bento 2014; IACHR 2015; Guadagnini, Antola, personal communication, as cited in Radi and Sardá-Chandiramani 2016). In addition, the challenges faced when bringing criminal cases to court include the negative discrimination and prejudices experienced by *travestis* and trans women when trying to achieve justice in an institutionally transphobic criminal justice system. They suffer secondary victimisation through their characters being discredited which negates their voices being heard. Thus, they are constructed as victims who cannot be empathised with unlike the attackers whose actions may be perceived as being morally justified. Thus, *travestis* and trans women are often constructed as being suspects as opposed to complainants or witnesses. This results in a lack of confidence in the police or criminal justice system to take their case seriously and effectively prosecute it, particularly if the complainant is involved in sex work. Furthermore, where the perpetrators are police officers, this can negatively affect those officers who are actively trying to solve the case and put their lives at risk (Gilardi, personal communication, April 2016 as cited in Radi and Sardá-Chandiramani). News agencies can also exacerbate the trauma of the crime by disclosing the masculine birth name of *travestis* and transsexuals reinforcing negative stereotypes about these communities (Bento 2014; Antola, personal communication, April 2016 as cited in Radi and Sardá-Chandiramani 2016). Next, First Nation Aboriginal trans people, their identity, culture and experiences of transphobic violence are examined.

First Nation Third Gender People

Aboriginal Transgender Identities and Culture

There are two groups which are unique to Australia, and they are (i) *brotherboys* and (ii) *sistergirls*; integral features of their self-definition within these categories are kinship and their cultural identification. Hence, why '*sistergirl*' and '*brotherboy*' are used by Australian support groups, in order to denote inclusion and focus attention on indigenous Australian trans women and trans men, respectively (see Kerry 2014). However, the term '*sistergirl*' is not universally used or applied in a consistent manner. Nevertheless, this term is deemed acceptable for those from 'traditional or semi-traditional communities'. Those *sistergirls* who came from an urban background emphasised that for them, *sistergirls* were individuals with 'transgender qualities' (Costello and Nannup 1999, p. 6). Kerry (2014) states that '[w]ithin traditional communities transphobia is linked directly to the liminal social status of *sistergirls*. Although the term and social role of a "*sistergirl*" offers a way of articulating experiences and needs that are distinct from cisgendered indigenous and non-indigenous Australians, their place in traditional communities is "precarious"' (p. 183).

Regarding the prevalence of transphobic violence within this indigenous community, research suggests that transphobia is a key feature in the lives of transgender Australians with 73.5% of trans men and 69.7% of trans women reporting being harassed through verbal violence. Moreover, 29.4% of trans men and 46.9% of trans women were subjected to threats of violence. In addition, physical attacks were reported by 11% of trans men and 18.2% of trans women. Furthermore, rape or sexual assault was reported by 17.6% of trans men and 13.6% of trans women (Kerry 2014). Unfortunately, no details were provided regarding the context or perpetrator(s). 'The most common forms of violence perpetrated against the *sistergirl* community appeared to be physical, sexual assault and rape' (see Costello and Nannup 1999, p. 8). It is therefore interesting to note that according to Costello and Nannup (1999) that due to violence being condoned within indigenous communities, that the violence experienced by *sistergirls* was also normalised.

Traditional communities are based on a rigid gender binary with regard to the roles assigned to women and men. Therefore, '...what is distinctly experienced by indigenous transgender Australians is racism within the wider Australian communities (including queer communities) and transphobia within traditional indigenous communities' (Kerry 2014, p. 185). Next, indigenous communities' treatment of trans people within First Nation Native American culture is examined below.

Native American Transgender Identities

'Queer indigeneous people have been under the surveillance of white colonial heteropatriarchy since contact' (Driskill et al. 2011, p. 212). The colonial influence was most keenly felt by First Nation Native Americans which will be referred to here. Within First Nation Native American culture, trans people are referred to as being two-spirited people; previously, the colonial term '*berdache*' was used by anthropologists and researchers which is considered insulting by First Nation (Native American) people across North America (see Besnier 1996; Epple 1998; Kessler and McKenna 1978) and indigenous people of Canada—as they were being labelled rather than being asked how they self-identified. The term '*berdache*' is of Persian origin and understood to historically mean 'kept boy' (see p. 26). Kessler and McKenna (1978) also discuss the '*berdache*' who originate from aboriginal North America. While Hill (as cited in Nanda 1990) uses the colonial term '*berdache*' to refer to intersex people within the Navaho tribe in the Mohave. These individuals received social sanctions for assuming a gender role which was opposite to their natal sex or assigned gender at birth. Some *berdache* were homosexual, others transvestic or were both transvestites and intersex; the term '*berdache*' is no longer used and is referenced here purely for contextual reasons and to highlight its inappropriateness. Two alternate gender categories identified are *alyha* (transvestite homosexuals) and *hwame* (lesbians) (Nanda 1990). *Alyha* self-identify in pre-adolescence by engaging in activities and dress of the opposite gender. For example, instead of learning to ride and hunt, some boys demonstrate a preference for playing with dolls, engaging in domestic chores and wishing to wear a 'female bark shirt' rather than a 'male breech clout'. Their families are ambivalent about their behaviour, but initially try to encourage them to engage in more male-orientated activities, and if these efforts are unsuccessful, they will initiate them via a transvestite ceremony whereby they will wear feminine clothing. Transvestite songs would also be sung. They will dance as women do and once confirmed as *alyha,* taken to a river to bathe (this could be symbolic of a rebirth into the female gender), given girls' skirts and thus their gender status is confirmed on a permanent basis. As *alyha* she will not take on a female lineage name. However, she will take a husband, engage in oral and anal intercourse and refer to her penis as a clitoris, her testes as labia majora and anus as a vagina. *Alyha* are also considered better housewives than women which increased their attractiveness as spouses. *Alyha* will also go to extreme lengths to mirror women's biological cycle regarding menstruation (e.g., using a stick to scratch between their legs till they bled), and even mimic pregnancy. Pregnancy is faked by simulating the bump with extra clothing; a potion is ingested to cause stomach pains and through defecation 'a still birth' is simulated and then buried. The couple would then cut their hair short in mourning. Although *alyha* were not teased within the tribe as they were seen as quite powerful, their husbands were teased for marrying them. Another aspect of their prescribed role related to mysticism and healing powers as they were perceived to be potent shamans particularly for curing conditions such as STDs like syphilis (see Nanda 1990).

Hwame were like shamans, thus like the *hijra* there was a mystical/spiritual element to their role. They were, however, less accepted than *alyha*. But, *hwame* were considered excellent providers, but had unstable marriages. If they married a pregnant woman, they could claim paternity of child as sexual intercourse with a pregnant woman could change the paternity of the child according to the Mohave. Some *hwame* took up their man–woman status after giving birth to a child. However, in contrast with the *alyha*, their gender identity preferences were for male activities, masculine modes of dress and they rejected the female alternatives; these behaviours also presented in childhood (Devereaux cited in Lang 1998). The *hwame* were similar to the *alyha* in that their wives were teased. Nevertheless, where they differ is that unlike the *alyha* who were socially accepted, *hwame* occupied a much more precarious position within the tribe. As at one level, their alternate gender was accepted with regard to the carrying out activities of the opposite gender and dressing in accordance with their male role. Nonetheless, this acceptance is suggested as being quite superficial as their wives were verbally harassed as stated above. Furthermore, the *hwame* despite their shamanic role which appears to act as a protective characteristic for *alyha*, does not offer them the same protection. *Hwame* were therefore '...exposed to actual verbal and physical assaults, and occasionally even raped by men' according to Devereaux who 'described the rapists as 'practical jesters', where '...a drunken *hwame* was forced to have sexual intercourse with several men seems astonishingly insensitive' (as cited in Lang 1998, p. 294). Thus, in accordance with Lang's anthropological writings regarding the gender ambivalence of *hwame* and *alyha*, the institutionalisation of gender variance did not appear to explicitly challenge either the cultural norms of heterosexual marriage or the gender division of labour regarding the appropriate roles of men and women. Therefore, whether women–men/men–women entered into relationships with men or women, they were still culturally constructed as heterogender (see Lang 1998). The transgender identities discussed above where the opposite gender role to the person's natal gender is adopted with regard to their mode of dress and gendered activities undertaken contrast with that of the *'nadle'* or '*nádleehé*'. The *nadle* identity blurs the gender boundaries and provides a much more fluid presentation of their gender regarding their physical appearance, and sexual orientation which is also less well defined.

The *nadle* who were part of the Navajo tribe present with personality features that are ascribed to the other gender but there is ambivalence with regard to sexual identity, and the discrepancy between their physical appearance and behaviour results in dual sexuality which presents as physical ambivalence. 'The status of nadle is an ambivalent, nonmasculine and nonfeminine gender status which requires either physical or psychic-physical ambivalence' (Lang 1998, p. 69). She cited Hill when discussing *nadle* and stated he was not clear as to whether they were male- or female-bodied or intersex; but, she suggests that it is most likely he was referring to male-bodied or intersex people. The Navajo stated that *nadle* were better women than natal women, as they were guardians of traditionally gendered activities and have access to all female-oriented activities but were excluded from male-specific ones of hunting and warfare. In contrast, the *winkte* (female-to-male) of the Lakota tribe dedicated themselves to women's work but also hunted. Thus, they engaged in combined gendered activities and took a much more flexible approach to the expression of their gender identity. *Winkte* were understood to have supernatural power to bestow secret names. These trans men are similar to *hwame* only with regard to their natal gender and their self-presentation as the opposite gender. Although they engaged in specific specialist occupations within the context of their masculine gender role, they dedicated themselves to women's work (Lang 1998). However, this adoption of specialist male roles was the choice of the individual as to whether they wished to engage in these as well as participate in men's everyday work activities. Depending on their occupational specialisms and whether they were within the feminine sphere of responsibilities or they were activities which could be undertaken irrespective of sex; there was more flexibility in this sense within the Lakota tribe in this regard. According to Lang (1998), the Oglala Lakota winkte had an additional social role whereby they were considered good match-makers. There were no reports here of *winkte* being subjected to overt violence because of their transgender presentation, this does not mean that such violence may not have occurred but may instead be reflective of researchers not asking such questions. Next, the transgender identies within the Zuni tribe of First Nation Native Americans are discussed.

Zuni *lhamana* are initiated into the ko'tikili when masculine characteristics or oppositional gender identity preferences first present. Young males did not have to choose this gender role until puberty even if prior to this they showed a preference for female clothing and tasks. However, *lhamana* occupy a gender ambivalent role that has some parallels with the *winkte*. They engaged in women's activities such as weaving textiles and baskets and demonstrated a mastery of these skills as well as being expert plasterers which was more of a male ascribed activity (see Parsons as cited in Lang 1998). They also carried out the most difficult labour intensive women's tasks. Again, here there was no discussion of any violence experienced by those who undertook this role so it may suggest that there was widespread social acceptance within the tribe of this flexible gender role. Nevertheless, evidence to confirm or reject such speculations is unavailable and thus more research is required in this regard. In the next section, transgender identities are explored in Tahiti, Tonga, Indonesia, Africa, Korea, China, Japan and Vietnam.

Transgender Identities within other International Communities

Trans people are referred to in Tahitian and contemporary Hawaiian terms as *māhū* and Samoan *fa'afāfine* '(in the fashion of a woman)' (Besnier 1996, p. 286). Thus, '[i]n Samoa a *fafine* is a woman, [and] a *tane* is a man or husband…' (McMullin 2011, p. 85). However, McMullin does not name what Samoan women who dress as men are called, this may be because evidence of their visibility is rare. The reader will note that throughout the discussion of trans people within these indigenous communities, disproportionate attention is often given to men who identify with the opposite gender, while their female counterparts are either considered not to exist or given cursory attention in the literature. When they are discussed as in the case of the *hwame* above, it is noteworthy that they were condoned targets for transphobic sexual violence.

In Tonga, the term used is *fakaleiti* (borrowed from the English word 'lady') or *fakafefine*. Whereas the Tuvaluans use *pinapinaaine* of Gilbertese origin (Besnier 1996). Nanda (1990) suggests that in Tahitian culture, a third gender role that of the māhū is found. They are like some of the *hijra* as they are not castrated, they also do not cohabit, but live and dress as women, speak with a feminine voice, engage in traditional female employment, demonstrate a mastery of certain handicrafts and also sing with women. The māhū also do not wear facial hair (Morrison as cited in Levy 1973, Nanda 1990). Historical accounts of Captain Bligh of the Bounty ship recounts how the genitalia of māhū were examined and found to be underdeveloped male genitalia that had been tucked in. It is noteworthy that māhū people were treated with the *'same esteem and respect as women according to Bligh'* (as cited in Levy 1973, pp. 130–131, see Nanda 1990). In order to mimic heterosexual intercourse more closely, it was noted that historically interfemoral intercourse was practised not anal intercourse. According to Tahitian cultural traditions, the māhū fellate the man he has had sex with and ingests his semen as it was understood to bestow strength, the *māhū* were also believed to have exceptional strength. There were rigid heteronormative gender roles described with regard to sexual acts whereby the *māhū's* partner is always the recipient of oral intercourse and never the provider of fellatio. The *māhū's* partner is also described as the passive partner never the active one (Nanda 1990). There are conflicting accounts about the homosexual activities of the *māhū* with some Tahitian men stating it was central to their role but others denying this, and younger men refuting this rejection. Nevertheless, Nanda suggests that the *māhū* are not defined solely by their sexual orientation. The relationship between the *māhū* and their partner is differentiated from a homosexual couple as the *māhū* are perceived as women. Tahitian culture defines the Western import of 'homosexuality' as *raerae* which means 'sex-role reversal' and pertains to sodomy and applies to a role reversal between male and female sexual relations (see Levy as cited in Nanda 1990). Each district has one *māhū*, the person volunteers for this role by being willing to dress and engage in the activities of a woman (domestic chores, childcare, etc. in public, or as in another district associating with adolescent girls, walking arm in arm, usually an activity only participated in by homosexual males (see Levy as cited in Nanda, p. 136). However, Nanda's account lacks clarity as to whether undertaking the role of *māhū* is due to being intersex or the possession of any genital abnormalities, but her reading of Levy's work explicitly states that Tahitians do not believe that one can 'change their sex' and it is possible to revert to non-*māhū* masculine status. Therefore, there is a fluidity here that again is particularly reflective of the *xanith*. There also seems to be a social acceptance of this role although like the hijra (see Nanda 1990) young men do harass *māhū* and may ridicule them despite boasting about sleeping with them and emphasising their promiscuous nature (Besnier 1996).

Park (email communication as cited in Feinberg 1996) identifies the existence of trans people known as *'basaja'* on the Indonesian island of Sulawesi (Celebes). In Korea, trans males are known as the *'mundang'* who was a shaman or sorcerer, whereas in Ancient China, the *shih-niang* wore a combination of male and female dress together with religious apparel. In addition, in Okinawa, Japan, certain shamen participated in male-to-female ceremonies known as *winagu-nati* ('becoming female') (see p. 45), while in African cultures, female-to-male (FTM) shamans co-exist with male-to-female (MTF) shamans, for example, in the Lugbara tribe, a MTF person is called an *okule* and FTM person is called an *agule*. In South Africa, the Zulu too initiated both FTM and MTF *isangoma*. MTF shamans also existed as part of traditional life of the First Nation peoples of the Arctic Basin; for example, Inuit FTMs serve the White Whale Woman, a spiritual being who is gender flexible according to accounts of her being transformed into a man or a 'woman–man' (Boas as cited in Feinberg 1996). Thus, the common characteristic amongst the majority of trans people across different cultures is the shared mystical or spiritual element of their persona which was sometimes enough to protect them from transphobic violence and gender-based harassment.

According to the writings of Feinberg (1996) who suggests that irrespective of which culture, there is a persistent spiritual connection with regard to the role of trans people, however, this is uniquely absent in Western cultures. With regard to the latter, transsexualism is encompassed within the transgender status and is not defined as an alternative or 'third gender'. However, for the *hijra,* the female and male signifiers of 'male and female' are similarly constructed to Western gender signifiers of maleness, as the phallus and the child bearing capacity of women (possession of a vagina). With regard to the *xanith,* the male signifier is male potency and the active sexual position being taken in intercourse, whereas with the *alyha* and *māhū,* the presence or absence of male genitalia does not impact on their presenting in a female role as long as they dress and engage in female domestic-related activities (the former also taking on the female passive role in sexual intercourse).

Traditionally, in Western culture there is a perceived permanence with regard to one's gender identity and that even when a person transitions to confirm their subjective gender identity; the expectation is they will not revert back to their natal gender identity. This is highlighted in Chap. 3 when discussing legislation in relation to gender identity. However, there is more fluidity and public acceptance with regard to gender identity in indigenous cultures as seen above. For example, the *hijra* (prior to emasculation), the *māhū* and *xanith* allow individuals the opportunity to revert back to their natal gender identity should they wish to do so. Thus, the importance of physical and biological characteristics lies in gender attribution and may combine in bearded women, penile women and vaginaed men. The complexity of gender attributions can be further highlighted by pre-operative transsexuals being sperm donors and also socially women. '…[W]e assert that not only is gender attribution far from a simple inspection process, but gender attribution forms the foundation for understanding other components of gender, such as gender role (behaving like a female or male) and gender identity (feeling like a female or male)' (Kessler and McKenna 1978, p. 2). By confirming one's internalised gender identity through hormone therapy, feminisation surgery and less so by undergoing gender confirmation surgery, trans people's internal gender identity and external gender presentation may be aligned. This reinforces the gender binary and associated cultural stereotypes rather than challenging them and facilitating the development of a 'third gender' as discussed above in indigenous cultures. Just as there are parallels regarding the mystical and spiritual aspects of the transgender identity across non-Western cultures, so too are there overlaps between the restricted access to occupational spheres which increase transgender peoples' vulnerability to transphobic violence and harassment. For example, when trans women are economically forced to engage in 'survival sex' or sex work irrespective of culture. Examples include the *hijra* and *travesti*, and similarly transgender sex workers in other territories such as America (Boles and Elifson 1994; Weinberg et al. 1999). *Xaniths* present female characteristics in their sex work role and this occupational context has parallels with the perceived promiscuity of Polynesian gender liminal people. Engagement in sex work due to restricted employment opportunities in indigenous cultures also occurs in Western countries, whereby trans women's risk and vulnerability to violence are therefore increased. However, Polynesian gender liminal people have more work options available to them. The problem with researching transgender people in non-Western contexts according to Nanda (1990) is the ethnocentric tone which unhelpfully projects Western gender concepts onto other cultures. Furthermore, Roen (2001) also emphasised that ethnic diversity in transgender communities continues to be ignored as reflected by the predominant 'Whiteness' of transgender research. There have thus been renewed calls for conducting more intersectional research with regard to transgender socially constructed identities (see Nagoshi and Brzuzy 2010) and how ethnicity, class and socio-economic status as well as gender and sexual orientations can intersect to exacerbate discriminatory responses at an institutional level and increase trans people's vulnerability to violence as a result of hazardous occupations being undertaken due to limited employment opportunities.

In the next chapter, transphobic violence is examined with regard to its prevalence, nature and type on a national and international scale. In addition, the perceived 'naturalisation' of the gender binary is discussed referencing the different theoretical perspectives reinforcing and challenging this 'norm'. The reader is also encouraged to consider whether the approaches taken to accept trans people are as conceptually advanced as suggested by these progressive countries or could more be learned from indigenous societies' adoption of gender flexibility as being normative.

References

Agrawal, A. (1997). Gendered bodies: The case of the 'Third gender' in India. *Contributions to Indian Sociology, 31,* 273–296.

Besnier, N. (1996). *Polynesian gender liminality through time and space third sex, third gender: Beyond sexual dimorphism in culture and history* (pp. 285–328). Cambridge, MA: MIT.

Boles, J., & Elifson, K. W. (1994). The social organization of transvestite prostitution and AIDS. *Social Science and Medicine, 39,* 85–93.

Costello, M., & Nannup, R. (1999). *Report of the first National Indigenous Sistergirl Forum: a forum for all indigenous people who identify as a sistergirl or who have transgender qualities: Magnetic Island, Queensland, July 17–20.* Darlinghurst, N.S.W.: AIDS Trust of Australia Queensland AIDS Council.

Driskill, Q.-L., Finley, C., Gilley, B. J., & Morgensen, S. L. (2011). Introduction. In Q.-L. Driskill, C. Finley, B. J. Gilley, & S. L. Morgensen (Eds.), *Queer indigenous studies: Critical interventions in theory, politics and literature* (pp. 1–28). Tucson: University of Arizona Press.

Epple, C. (1998). Coming to terms with Navaho Nádleehí: A critique of Berdache, 'Gay', 'alternate gender', and 'two-spirt'. *American Ethnologist, 25,* 267–290.

Feinberg, L. (1996). *Trans gender warriors.* Boston: Beacon Press.

Kahn, S. I., Hussain, M. I., Parveen, S., Bhuiyan, M. I., Gourab, G., Sarker, G. F., et al. (2009). Living on the extreme margins: Social exclusion of the transgender population (Hijra) in Bangladesh. *Journal of Health Population & Nutrition, 4,* 441–451.

Kalra, S. (2012). The eunuchs of India: An endocrine eye opener. *Indian Journal of Endocrinology and Metabolism, 16*(3), 377–380. Retrieved form http://doi.org/10.4103/2230-8210.95676, http://www.ncbi.nlm.nih.gov/pmc/articles/PMC3-354843/?report=printable.

Kang, B. D. (2012). Kathoey "In Trend": Emergent genderscapes, national anxieties and the re-signification of male-bodied effeminacy in Thailand. *Asian Studies Review, 36,* 475–494.

Kerry, S. C. (2014). Sistergirls/brotherboys: The status of indigenous transgender Australians. *International Journal of Transgenderism, 15*(3–4), 173–186.

Kessler, S., & McKenna, W. (1978). *Gender: An ethnomethodological approach.* New York: Wiley.

Kimmel, M. S. (2008). *The gendered society* (3rd ed.). Oxford: Oxford University Press.

Kulick, D. (1998). *Travesti: Sex, gender and culture among Brazilian transgendered prostitutes.* Chicago: University of Chicago Press.

Lang, S. (1998). *Men as women, women as men: Changing gender in Native American cultures.* Austin: University of Texas Press.

McMullin, D.T. (2011). 'Fa'afafine notes; On Tagaloa, Jesus, and Nafanua'. In Q-L. Driskill, C. Finley, B. J. Gilley & S. L. Morgensen (Eds.), *Queer indigeneous studies: Critical interventions in theory, politics and literature* (pp. 81–94). Tucson: University of Arizona Press.

Monro, S. (2010). Towards a sociology of gender diversity: The Indian and UK cases. In S. Hines & T. Sanger (Eds.), *Transgender identities: Towards a social analysis of gender diversity* (pp. 242–258). London: Routledge.

Nagoshi, J. L., & Brzuzy, S. (2010). Transgender theory: Embodying research and practice. *Afilia: Journal of Women and Social Work, 25*(4), 431–443.

Nanda, S. (1990). *Neither man nor woman.* Belmont: Wadsworth.

Radi, B., & Sardá-Chandiramani, A. (2016). Travesticide/transfemicide: Coordinates to think crimes against travestis and transwomen in Argentina. [Online Publication].

Roen, K. (2001). Transgender theory and embodiment: The risk of racial marginalisation. *Journal of Gender Studies, 10*(3), 253–263.

United Nations Development Fund (UNDP). (2010). *Hijras/Transgender women in India: HIV, human rights and social exclusion.* New Delhi: Author.

Weinberg, M. S., Shaver, F. M., & Williams, C. J. (1999). Gendered sex work in the San Franciso Tenderloin. *Archives of Sexual Behaviour, 28*(6), 503–521.
Wetsiriyanan, T., Chamruspanth, V., & Srisontisuk, S. (2016). The transgender's sexual identity construction in a cultural practice community: A case study of the Ganesh Chaturthi ceremony. *The Social Sciences, 11*(5), 589–594.
Wikan, U. (1982). *Behind the veil in Arabia: Women in Oman*. Baltimore: John Hopkins University Press.
Winter, S., Rogando-Sasot, S., & King, M. (2007). Transgendered women of the Philippines. *International Journal of Transgenderism, 10*(2), 79–90.

2

Transphobic Hate Crime on a National and International Scale

Abstract The extent, nature, type and context of transphobic hate violence are discussed here. First, theoretical perspectives and debates regarding transgender-based violence perpetrated for gender deviancy are examined. Second, the neglect of ethnic diversity within the available literature resulting in quite a polarised perspective on transgender identities is highlighted. Third, the prevalence of transphobic violence on a national and international scale is provided. Fourth, the nature and type of transphobic hate violence are analysed by exploring the different types such as verbal, physical and sexual violence. Fifth, the impact of gendered territories and access to safe spaces are also discussed in relation to how the intersectional characteristics of a trans person may increase their vulnerability to hate crime. Case studies are used to illustrate these points.

Keywords Prevalence · Theoretical perspectives · Verbal violence
Physical violence · Sexual violence · Gendered space · Vulnerability
Case studies

J. Jamel, *Transphobic Hate Crime*, Palgrave Hate Studies,
https://doi.org/10.1007/978-3-319-57879-8_2

'Some members of [...] society ridicule gender-variant people for being 'different' and they may even be hostile. Even from police, they face physical and verbal abuse, forced sex, extortion of money and materials; and arrests on false allegations. The absence of protection from police means ruffians find Hijras/TG people as easy targets for extorting money and as sexual objects' (UNDP 2010, p. 8). In Chap. 1, diverse cultural perspectives were explored with regard to different societal responses to gender diversity being affected by geographic and historical influences. These influences continue to inform research findings such as the 'Whiteness' of the theoretical perspectives and research referred to below. In this chapter, it is suggested that the intersectionality of victims can increase the likelihood of their victimisation and exacerbate its impact as a result of institutional discrimination (see Tyra Hunter's case below).

From birth, as members of society, we are socialised into particular gender roles determined by the evidence of primary sexual characteristics such as external genitalia. Sex Role Theory (Parsons and Bale 1956) latterly known as Gender Role Theory asserts what is appropriate 'masculine' (e.g. strong, assertive, aggressive) and 'feminine' (e.g. submissive, passive, nurturing) behaviours. Social agents consisting of the family, education, peers and occupational culture provide the socialising influences resulting in gender conformity. However, for those who fail to adhere to gender role norms such as gender non-conforming, non-binary gender and transgender individuals, sanctions are thus perpetrated by transphobic hate crime offenders. These offenders are threatened by the perceived destabilising effect of non-binary genders which threatens their traditional and heteronormative conceptualisations of gender roles. 'Heteronormativity is defined as the set of norms that make heterosexuality seem natural or right and that organize homosexuality as its binary opposite' (Corber and Valocchi 2003, p. 4). The motivations of hate crime offenders will be discussed in Chap. 4 when discussing the victim–offender relationship.

Perry (2003) suggested that transphobic hate crime offenders' objective is to send a warning 'message' directly to the victim but also indirectly to wider society. Transphobic hate crime offenders reinforce conformity to people's natal gender through the violent sanctions perpetrated against perceived gender 'deviants', also reinforcing the marginalisation and historical subordination of vulnerable communities. Trans people's victimisation and the response to it may also be by negatively impacted upon by the multiple ethnicities and gender characteristics of victims. Bornstein (1994) refers to these hate crime offenders as 'gender terrorists', for example those who raped and murdered Brandon Teena (a trans male) her friend Lisa Lambert and Lisa's friend Philip DeVine in Falls City, Nebraska in 1993. Halberstam (2003) notes the importance of this case lies in its raising the issue of the particular vulnerabilities to violence experienced by queer (encompassing trans, gay and lesbian identities) youths within rural North America. She suggests that the motivation for the homicide of Brandon Teena is that his gender presentation, and treatment of his girlfriends in a sensitive and respectful manner emphasising his middle-class background and more subtle performance of masculinity undermined the working-class men in this rural community and their macho treatment of females. It is therefore suggested that the performance of gender roles within this provincial community is in accordance with traditional masculine values where men must present as the aggressor, be unemotional and act out in a hypermasculine manner. Thus, reinforcing a rigid gender dichotomy which does not acknowledge the possibility of non-binary or third gender identities; as to recognise the existence of multiple gender identities would be perceived as a threat with regard to the potential destabilisation of the 'naturalised' gender dichotomy.

Bornstein (1994), however, constructs a third space external to society's gender dichotomy for self-identified 'gender outlaws'. The case of Gwen Araujo who was beaten and strangled to death when her transgender status was discovered after she had consensual sex with several men at a party (Lloyd 2013). Trans people are not only victims of transphobic violence but also discrimination in housing, employment, in prison (see Jamel 2017), and health care such as in the case of Tyra Hunter. She was a pre-operative trans woman who was the victim of a road traffic accident and when the Fire Department EMTs realised her transgender status during the assessment of her injuries they discontinued treatment. They then ridiculed her (this could be deemed verbal and psychological violence), this mistreatment was continued at the hospital where she was not treated in a competent or swift manner considering the severity of her injuries, this medical negligence led to her death (see Fox 1999).

The complexity of transphobic hate crime is further illustrated when we examine the multiple layers of the vulnerability of victimisation based on ethnicity, class and sexual orientation. These exacerbating factors result in the increased likelihood of victimisation but are also absent in theoretical perspectives. For example, Roen (2001) emphasised the 'Whiteness' of transgender theory, suggesting it needs to become more racialised; this is reflected in her use of examples of acceptance within Maori culture, where gender liminality (the recognition of a 'third gender') is normative. This perspective allows for gender fluidity and facilitation of gender non-conformity or non-binary genders. This perspective also has implications regarding the medicalisation of transgenderism and how this may be negotiated as this is often reinforced within legislation. For example, the language used in the GRA 2004 in England enshrines a binary gender as one must live as one's acquired gender until death. Links between the gender binary, socialisation and legislation will be discussed in more detail in Chap. 3.

Hate crime incidents are more likely to involve individuals who are **'Crossing'**, living visibly as a transgender person as opposed to **'Passing'** (assimilating in order to conform to society's norms) as their acquired gender (Eliot and Roen 1998). The ability to pass is often based on appearance and body type, with less attention being given to the influence of ethnicity and class. However, Bettcher (2007) states that even those individuals whose characteristics may be read as male can be mediated by a good quality wig, nice clothes and beauty treatments to enable them to successfully pass. Compared to those of lower socio-economic status who cannot afford such 'aids' and are consequently easily read and subject to harassment and physical violence. Intersectionality of ethnicity, class and socio-economic status thus impact on the level of visibility in society and their ability to 'pass' or 'transition' successfully. These intervening factors draw on Bourdieu's (2010) constructs of social, cultural and economic capital which can facilitate successful 'passing' and diminish symbolic, physical, emotional, psychological and sexual violence.

Prevalence of Transphobic Hate Crime

According to research, the extent of transphobic victimisation is that three in four trans people are targeted annually. Furthermore, that the prevalence of transphobic victimisation which trans men and women experience does not significantly differentiate between them (see Whittle et al. 2007). However, Kelley's (2009) research found a higher percentage of trans women were victims of transphobic hate crime. This may be due to trans women's increased visibility compared with trans men. In addition, trans men may also be less likely to contact victim services about transphobic or homophobic incidents. Homophobic hate crimes according to the 'OSCE, EU Fundamental Rights Agency and Human Rights First, are legislated against by *"13 EU member States (Belgium, Denmark, Estonia, Finland, France, Germany, Ireland, the Netherlands, Portugal, Romania, Spain, Sweden, the United Kingdom) as well as Andorra, Canada, Croatia, and since very recently, the USA, have legislation which addresses hate motivated attacks or crimes motivated by sexual orientation, either as a specific offence or as an aggravating circumstance in the commission of a crime. Apart from the United States and Scotland in the United Kingdom, there is no State that makes a specific reference in its criminal law to hate crime based on gender identity"'* (Swiebel and van der Veur 2009, p. 493). The situation regarding the legal recognition of hate crime based on gender has now changed across some of these territories and these will be discussed later. Transphobic hate crime can range in severity and involve multiple incidents on a daily basis (Stotzer 2009). In 2010, there were 357 hate crimes targeting the trans community recorded in England, Wales and Northern Ireland (Smith et al. 2012). In London alone in 2011, the number of reported transphobic hate crimes was between 60 and 90 (Guttierz-Cooper, personal communication, 2011, personal correspondence). In London, for the period of 2012/2013, the police recorded 50 transphobic hate crimes, however, as stated above this is an enormous underrepresentation of the actual prevalence of this type of crime according to anecdotal evidence (see Antjoule 2013). In addition, Yeung (2016) suggests that the number of hate crimes reported to the police has almost tripled since 2011 when it was 215 to 582 in 2015.

There are also a number of inhibitors to the accurate recording of transphobic hate crime from the lack of recognition; for example, in some territories such as the USA, the Bureau of Justice Statistics only began including gender bias crimes in its hate crime statistics since 2010 (Sandholtz et al. 2013). Transgender victims of hate crimes are also less visible within statistics documenting hate crime as a consequence of the underreporting, and hence under-recording of this type of crime (Swiebel and van der Veur 2009). Complainants may therefore not receive an appropriate level of support if services are needs-directed. Also, a real or perceived lack of a sympathetic response from the police may be envisioned by victims of such hate crimes depending on their previous experiences of the policing response in this regard. In addition to this information is the fact that the low prosecution rate reinforces the lack of faith in the police response to this crime.

Inhibitors to Reporting

Reasons for not reporting include (i) mistrust of the police, (ii) lack of confidence in the police investigating the incident, (iii) disillusionment with the police's ability to do something about it, (iv) fear of a transphobic police response and (v) fear of reprisal or being outed to family or neighbours. According to the College of Policing (2014), crimes that should be recorded as transgender hate crimes are where the victim or other person perceives the motivation (partially or completely) as transphobia, or where this hostility was evident prior, during or post-offence. The victim may not be trans but be perceived as such or even be a friend or relative of the trans person. Recorded police statistics for the 2015–2016 period state that 858 (1%) of all hate crimes were directed against trans people (Corcoran and Smith 2016). Furthermore, it was noted that in 41 of the 43 police forces in England and Wales, transphobic hate crime was the 'least commonly recorded' hate crime (Corcoran et al. 2015). However, it should also be noted that a fifth of transphobic crimes occur in London despite only one in eight of the population living there (Antjoule 2013). In Ireland, TENI (2014) documented 32 transphobic incidents from assault to rape to property damage; however, only 15 of these were categorised as hate crimes. The respondents in this study were composed of the following gender groups: trans women (56%), female (41%) which included trans and cisgender-identified individuals. On the masculine spectrum, there were trans men (22%), male (6%), transgender (19%) and 'other' (13%) such as genderqueer or gender fluid. And, one participant identified as intersex. Regarding sexual orientation, over a quarter identified as lesbian (28%), a quarter were unsure of their sexual orientation and 22% identified as bisexual, gay (6%), heterosexual (6%), 'other', pansexual or queer (13%). The average age was 31, the age range of respondents was between 17 and 63 with the majority aged from 18 to 44 (TENI 2014). An additional barrier to reporting can be the perceived normalisation of these hate-motivated acts and consequently a failure to recognise them as crimes (FRA 2014; Kelley 2009).

The dark figure of unreported and unrecorded crimes is therefore particularly problematic with regard to ascertaining the extent of a hate crime because sexual orientation and gender-motivated hate crime particularly suffer from a lack of representation by both victims and the police. The British Crime Survey included questions on sexual orientation-motivated hate crime as recently as 2009–2010, and gender identity-based hate crime has been included in the rebranded Crime Survey for England and Wales in 2011–2012. The Association of Chief Police Officers (ACPO) stated that from January to December 2010 that of 48,127 crimes recorded in England, Wales and Northern Ireland, 357 of these were hate crimes targeting trans individuals (i.e. transphobic hate crimes) (Smith et al. 2012). This is quite a low figure when one considers that trans people may be subjected to verbal violence or hate speech on a daily basis.

It is also noteworthy that the FBI only began collecting statistics on transphobic hate crime as recently as 2013. This lack of recognition served to further increase the invisibility and marginalisation of this underserved community of trans people. The collection of officially recorded statistics on hate crime emphasises the increasing importance of transphobic hate crime, thus further raising awareness and facilitating improved assistance for victims through needs-directed services. According to the recent FBI statistics for the 2014–2015 period of the 109 victims of gender identity bias, 69 were victims of anti-transgender bias and 40 were victims of anti-gender non-conforming bias (FBI 2014). The difference between anti-transgender bias and anti-gender non-conforming bias is the following. Anti-transgender bias relates to a person being targeted because they identify as a gender different to that associated with their natal sex, for example a person who is born male but identifies as female and vice versa, or any individual who cross-dresses. Particular epithets may also be directed at them such as *'tranny'* and *'she-male'*. Anti-gender non-conforming bias relates to individuals who do not identify 100% as the other gender but feminise or masculinise their person to a limited extent. For example, a man identifying as male who wears male clothing but also wears make-up such as eyeliner, or nail polish, or a woman who identifies as female, wears female clothing but also wears a tie or other male attire. Invectives which may signify this type of crime include 'sissy' and 'tomboy' (FBI 2015). There is also a distinction between hate crime and bias-motivated crime, see below.

'The term bias more accurately reflects a preconceived prejudice toward members of a group characterized by certain attributes, whereas hate suggests a more personalized anger associated with a particular individual' (McDevitt et al. 2013, p. 108). The incidence of bias-motivated crime in the form of non-violent attacks is more difficult to research than violent equivalents (e.g. where a person is beaten and homophobic remarks are made throughout, there is physical evidence and 'public remarks' evidencing a hate-motivated attack (Wolff and Cokeley 2007). It has also been noted that marginalised communities (based on their ethnicity and/or sexual orientation) are reluctant to report crime to the police due to their belief that such agencies have a racial (Rice and Piquero 2005) and anti-gay bias, this is also frequently reinforced by their community's culture and media representations.

Thus, multiple vulnerabilities or intersectionalities regarding being a member of an ethnic minority, gay or lesbian, may further inhibit victims of transphobic hate crime from reporting crimes to the police. This lack of confidence in the police in sensitively handling their case is also a problem for the trans community (see Kelley 2009).

Types of Violence

Transphobic abuse can range from verbal harassment to physical assault, sexual assault and homicide. Witten (2003) found that 23% of hate-motivated attacks involved sexual harassment, 15% sexual abuse or attempted sexual abuse and 6% were subjected to rape as a result of their gender identity. Such extreme violence or even homicide is directed at trans females by males in a sexualised context motivated by anger at their 'gender deception'; this concept will be discussed later. Whereas research on trans men within the employment sector suggests that female colleagues gender them as being lesbian on the basis of their natal sex and thus respond using passive aggression by revealing their transgender identity in order to 'protect' their female colleagues from engaging in inadvertent homosexual acts (Schilt and Westbrook 2009). It is also of interest to examine the prevalence of transphobic violence in other cultures. For example, in 2007 a study stated in the past year, the percentage of those MSM (Men who have Sex with Men) and hijras (n = 75) subject to forced sex was 46%, physical abuse 44%, verbal abuse 56%, extortion 31%, and threat to life was 24% (UNDP 2010). As can be seen here, verbal violence is the most prevalent, thus, as aforementioned, it is unfortunately understandable how this hostile behaviour becomes normalised within trans peoples' daily lives. It was also noted that many trans individuals who identified as Lesbian, Gay or Bisexual (LGB) and were also occasionally subjected to homophobic hate crime (Kelley 2009).

Male perpetrators who had sexual intercourse with a person believed to be female, on discovering the person's trans female identity are concerned that consequently, they may be perceived as exhibiting homosexual tendencies due to the 'one-act rule of homosexuality' (Schilt and Westbrook 2009). Newspaper articles described that regarding the homicides of trans individuals, 56% of these were related to the transgender status of the victim (Clements-Nolle et al. 2006; Kenagy 2005; Moran and Sharpe 2004; Schilt and Westbrook 2009; Stotzer 2009; Turner et al. 2009; Witten 2003). The extremity of the physical and/or sexually violent response is in direct relation to the perpetrator's homophobia and their subscription to the 'one act rule of homosexuality' (i.e. the social perception that if a person engages in a same-sex sexual encounter just once then they are deemed homosexual). Anger is a motivation due to the alleged gender deception of the non-transgender male in this sexualised context resulting in a perceived homosexual encounter. Thus, an additional 5% of these documented cases involved the use of a trans panic defence in response to unsolicited sexual advances (Schilt and Westbrook 2009) and involved a non-transgender man killing a trans woman. This defence is grounded in the 'one-act rule of homosexuality' discussed above. In such cases, the non-transgender man is solicited for sex by a trans female and when he finds she has a penis, he retaliates with extreme violence for this perceived gender deception (Schilt and Westbrook 2009). Thus, trans women are framed as deceptive gay men due to their fraudulent seduction of 'innocent' non-transgender men. 'The extremity of men's responses shows the depth of the threat of transgender bodies to heteronormativity within sexual situations and the need to neutralize that threat through hyper-gendered reactions' (Schilt and Westbrook 2009, p. 458).

The following case of extreme transphobic violence illustrates the above points and was prosecuted as a hate crime. This case involved the aforementioned homicide of Gwen Araujo who at age 17 was killed at a party in California by four men in 2002. The trigger for her murder was the forced revelation that she had male genitalia and was thus accused of gender deception by the perpetrators as she had consensual sex with several of the men prior to her being physically beaten, strangled and buried in a shallow grave (see Steinberg cited in Lloyd 2013). A 'trans panic' defence was used by the four defendants stating their emotions were so intense on finding out her transgender identity they spontaneously responded using excessive violence. This defence was rejected. This was a complicated case and took two trials as the first was declared a mistrial. The second jury also was not willing to include hate crime enhancements to the sentencing despite the excessive violence and nature of the crime and the trigger for the killing (Lloyd 2013).

In North London in 2011 and 2015, there were two homicides of trans women. The first was Destiny Lauren a trans female sex worker who was murdered by Leon Fyle who was unknown to her, Fyle strangled her and considering the intimacy of this modus operandi it could be suggested that a sexual encounter may have taken place before he was aware of her transgender status. The former case of a trans female sex worker being murdered is one of those news stories which continually gets reported and reinforces certain stereotypes regarding trans women's occupations which does not recognise the limited access that trans women in particular face in the employment sector despite the Equality Act 2010, which will be discussed in the next chapter. The second case was the homicide of Chrissie Azzopardi a trans woman who was due to undergo gender confirmation surgery later that year. She was stabbed to death by her drug dealer Romy Maynard; the judge suggested there was a transphobic motive and that the trigger may have been his realisation of Chrissie's transgender status (www.thelawpages.com/court-cases/Romy-Maynard-12185-1.law).

However, the most-documented transgender homicides happen in Brazil (845) from 2008 to 2016, and 42% worldwide in 2016. Mexico was the second highest (245) for the same period, respectively; the occupations of those trans people who are targeted are usually sex workers and hairstylists (TGEU 2016). The cases in Brazil predominantly involved the victim's involvement in the sex work trade and/or drug misuse; thus, the risk of them being targeted is increased due to the clients who may frequent these areas. There were also cases of shootings and beatings such as that of Dias aged 33 who was a trans man (a carer and hospital escort) who on leaving a club was set upon and beaten to death. The cases above have been used to illustrate the excessive violence perpetrated in transphobic and hate-motivated homicides and also highlight the diversity of victims.

In Schilt and Westbrook's (2009) study, the context is key regarding the acceptance of trans men and women, in a social or work context (with top–down support) trans men and women may assimilate with their non-transgender male and female counterparts as long as they identify as heterosexual. However, in a private or sexualised context, transgressions of the gender and sexuality dichotomies are retaliated against by non-transgender males and females in a passive or actively aggressive manner. A related issue to this response is the fact that cisgender attraction to trans individuals is framed as pathological or fetishistic (Serano 2009). Kelley's (2009) research supports this by stating attacks on LGBT individuals are often transphobic in nature as the motivation is often because of the perceived gender deviancy (non-heteronormative) identity of the individual, e.g.

'effeminate' homosexual male or 'butch' lesbian. Thus, the main motivation was 'homophobia/transphobia' (58%). There is a greater concentration of research on trans females' transphobic victimisation and the different types of violence which they are subjected to and these are discussed next.

Thus, there is a gender differential in relation to the perpetration of sexual violence against members of the transgender community. For example, MTFs (69%) experienced higher rates of rape than FTMs (30%) (see Kenagy 2005). Approximately 50% of trans individuals report rape (coerced sexual intercourse) to the police (Stotzer 2009); there is little variance across studies regarding this figure (e.g., Clements-Nolle et al. 2006; Kenagy 2005). However, Reed et al. (2009) found that 2% of incidents involved sexual violence in their study. The term 'physical violence' includes a variety of acts, such as attempted bombings and abductions at the broad end of the spectrum compared to more narrow definitions encompassing physical beatings (Stotzer 2009). Witten (2003) stated that trans individuals were victims of hate-based muggings (29%) and beatings (39%). More recently, Whittle et al. (2007) found that 5% of trans individuals surveyed suffered physical abuse. While Clements-Noelle et al. (2006) found that 63% had been subjected to 'verbal gender victimisation'; whereas Witten (2003) stated that 23% had been victims of sexual harassment and 41% reported being followed or stalked. Also, Xavier (2000) reported that 18% of participants in this study experienced some kind of intimidation in addition to vandalism (4%) and blackmail or extortion (2%). Whereas Whittle et al. (2007) found that 19% suffered verbal harassment and 10% were targeted with threatening behaviour. Thus, it can be seen that the types of transphobic hate crime can vary significantly yet the research appears to focus on the narrower definition of physical violence; and sexual violence victimisation of trans people.

Feelings of Safety and the Location of Transphobic Attacks

Kenagy and Bostwick (2005) found that 56% of their respondents reported that being transgender made them feel unsafe and 43% of trans individuals felt uncomfortable in public. Furthermore, it is quite a grave finding that the perceived life expectancy of the transgender respondents in this study was described as follows: 40% felt they would have a shorter lifespan as a result of their gender identity (due to queer bashing, being killed by the police, the effects of hormones and HIV status). This fear of victimisation was also highlighted through respondents' level of spatial awareness and gendered safe spaces (e.g. in one case, a trans woman subjected to an aggravated sexual assault on leaving a nightclub, consequently changed her behaviour regarding what locations she felt safe to frequent) (see Moran and Sharpe 2004). However, few studies have included specific information regarding the location of transphobic attacks, although one study did find that '50% occurred at a private residence, 20% on public transport, 20% in public accommodation and 10% in the street or a public area' (Stotzer 2009, p. 174). Also, counter to public perceptions bias crimes do not tend to be perpetrated in 'cruising' areas or GLBT bars but according to Wolff and Cokely (2007) most were found to occur in their own homes (37%) which although a little higher, in the main supports previous research (see Comstock's [1991] study on homophobic crime; Kuehnle and Sullivan 2001). Nevertheless, some transphobic hate crime incidents did occur at GLBT venues (14%), at work (13%) and all of these cases warranted police attention. Other cases which involved direct contact with the police took place in the home, cars, public places (e.g. sidewalks), GLBT venues (13%) and public business or areas (11%) (Wolff and Cokely 2007). The cases in the next section evidence the extremity and excessive nature of the physical violence which may be perpetrated as part of a transphobic hate crime.

The motivation for homicide is frequently alleged 'gender deception' or the perceived threat of the trans person to the gender binary and heteronormative ideals which are more entrenched in Western society and particular macho or masculine tradition-based cultures on a global scale, e.g. Mexico, India, Italy, South America and Africa. For the period of 2008 to April 2016, the total number of reported homicides of trans people for all regions was 2115. Of these, 1654 trans and gender-diverse homicides were reported in Central and South America thus accounting for 78% of the global figures. Brazil (51%) and Mexico (15%) account for 66% of the entirety of reported murders in Central and South America. Providing a global context, 183 murders of trans and gender-diverse people in Asia (across 16 countries), North America (141), Canada (5), Europe (16 countries) (117), Africa (four countries) (10) and Oceania (four countries) (5) (TGEU 2016). These figures should be tempered by the recognition that these data may be limited by the diverse recording practices which may underestimate the prevalence of such homicides. The next section examines transphobic criminal victimisation that may occur more regularly within the daily lives of trans and gender non-conforming individuals.

Case Studies

The following case studies provide examples of verbal and physical violence perpetrated against trans people in their daily lives resulting in their fearing for their personal safety.

Paul Lewis

The victim within this case is Paul Lewis a trans man who was undergoing the process of gender reassignment. Paul Lewis contacted Stuart Davies (defendant) as he heard that [he] had an altercation with his fiancée—Amanda Miller. In the course of the phone call, the defendant threatened to kick Mr. Lewis' head in and called him "sick". Mr. Lewis and his fiancé then went to see a mutual friend. They were in the car when the defendant punched the windows several times, he then threatened to smash their heads in. Days later, Mr. Lewis was walking with another friend when he was again approached by the defendant. Again, a confrontation took place where Lewis was verbally abused because the defendant was transphobic and then physically assaulted. The defendant then threatened Mr. Lewis and stated that if the police were informed then he would get a sword from his house and decapitate him. Following CPS advice, the defendant was charged with making a menacing phone call (S127 Communications Act 2003), Section 4(1) Public Order Act and Battery. The offences were wholly motivated by the defendant's hatred of transgendered people and he admitted in interview that he was homophobic. The offences were all accompanied by abusive words used by the defendant expressing his dislike for gender change. These include describing Mr. Lee as "a thing" rather than a person "shime" (she/him), "lets see what kind of a man you are" and "you are sick". Both Mr. Lewis and his fiancé gave evidence at trial with the special measure of screens. During the trial, it came to light that the defendant's wife may have perverted the course of justice by trying to secure a false alibi. On this basis, the judge directed that the case be re-tried as key defence witnesses were discredited. The case was subsequently re-tried where the defendant changed his plea to guilty on Battery, which meant the couple were not required to give evidence for the second time. The Section 4 allegation was dropped. The defendant had previously pleaded guilty to making a menacing phone call. The defendant was [subsequently] sentenced to a Community Order for 18 months including 130 h [ours] of unpaid work in the community. [And,] £50 compensation was also ordered' (CPS 2008, p. 10).

Heather Williams

This case particularly [highlights] issues in relation to the potential infringement of the s22 Gender Recognition Act 2004 as the disclosure of any information would reveal the identity of the main victim (a transsexual woman) or her address which could have put her at risk of further intimidation. Ms. Williams was returning home from work and boarded an evening train. Mr. Braithewaite (Passenger 2) also boarded the train in the same carriage. Nearing the end of the journey, the defendant walked through the train and sat opposite Ms. Williams and tried to engage her in conversation. As Ms. Williams sensed a potential unwelcome situation and was in any case intending to alight at the next station, she did not wish to enter into a conversation with the defendant and told him that she had no time to talk as she was getting off at the next stop. The defendant continued in an aggressive and offensive and stated "I know you are a man". Ms. Williams did not want to discuss her gender identity with a stranger, but attempting to avoid argumentative confrontation, reluctantly replied "No, I am a transsexual woman". At this point, she gathered her possessions and moved to the exit doors. The defendant proceeded to follow her and verbally abuse her and another passenger who sought to intervene. At which point, the defendant pointed his finger in the face of the Mr. Braithewaite and said "Don't you fucking tell me what to do, you're one of them, bunch of queers". Ms. Williams then became concerned for her personal safety as the defendant moved to a position between her and the exit doors and continued to state "fuck off" and "dirty queers". As a result, she activated her personal attack alarm. When the train came to a halt Ms. Williams and Mr. Braithewaite alighted, along with the defendant. After Ms. Williams had been pursued down the station platform with the unwelcome tirade continuing, two Police Community Support Officers approached and positioned themselves between the defendant and Ms. Williams. The defendant continued to shout "She's a fucking man" in their presence and "fuck off you queers, fuck off out of England". He then tried to push one of the officers out of the way and kneed the other officer in the groin area. The defendant was restrained by one of the officers still shouting "you're a fucking queer" and "you fucking raped me". He was then restrained and arrested on suspicion of assault. Whilst in custody the defendant was further arrested on suspicion of Transphobic Section 4 Public Order. During interview, the defendant admitted his presence at the scene and to the offence. He admitted that he "can't stand" gay people and to being abusive with a homophobic content. The defendant was formally charged with an s.4a Public Order Act Transphobic offence and s.5 Public Order Act Homophobic Offence and assault on the PCSO' (CPS 2008, p. 12).

The above case studies both demonstrate the threatening effect of both verbal and physical violence which can be directed against trans people which we hear less about compared to the attention given to the extreme brutality of transphobic homicides. Nevertheless, these verbal attacks occur more regularly may be even on a daily basis and thus awareness needs to be raised and research carried out on the potentially psychological and physically damaging effect of such incidents.

In this chapter, the nature and type of transphobic hate crime have been discussed together with its prevalence and factors which mediate the likelihood of victimisation such as intersectionality. The intersectional characteristics consisting of ethnicity, gender, class, socio-economic status, etc. which can increase the vulnerability of trans and gender non-conforming people to hate crime victimisation and the impact these have on their recovery and resilience. The lack of faith and confidence in the police response to hate crime and the impact that this has on the reporting of this crime were also considered and this subject will be returned to later on. Theoretical perspectives were also referred to as rigid constructions of gender are socialised as being normative; also in societies with this traditional binary-gendered landscape, certain people (hate crime offenders) experience cognitive dissonance when faced with individuals who present as one gender, but who may possess the genitalia as the opposite gender. Religion also reinforces the binary gender structure of society, societal attitudes and law thus shaping legislation. It is therefore not until recent history that legislation has been passed regarding the protection and rights of trans people, which will be discussed in the next chapter.

References

Antjoule, N. (2013). *The hate crime report: Homophobia, biphobia and transphobia in London*. London: GALOP.

Bettcher, T. M. (2007). Evil deceivers and make-believers: On transphobic violence and the politics of illusion. *Hypatia, 22*(3), 43–65.

Bornstein, K. (1994). *Gender outlaw: On men, women and the rest of us*. New York: Routledge.

Bourdieu, P. (2010). *Distinction: A social critique of the judgment of taste*. London: Routledge.

Clements-Nolle, K., Marx, R., & Katz, M. (2006). Attempted suicide among transgender persons: The influence of gender-based discrimination and victimization. *Journal of Homosexuality, 51*(3), 53–69.

College of Policing. (2014). *Hate crime operational guidance*. Coventry: Author.

Comstock, G. D. (1991). *Violence against lesbians and gay men*. New York: Columbia University Press.

Corber, R. J., & Valocchi, S. (2003). *Queer studies: An interdisciplinary reader*. Oxford: Blackwell.

Corcoran, H., & Smith, K. (2016). *Hate crime, England and Wales 2015/16*. London: Home Office.

Corcoran, H., Lader, D., & Smith, K. (2015). *Hate crime, England and Wales 2014/2015*. London: Home Office.

CPS. (2008). *Homophobic and transphobic crime toolkit: Good practice and lessons learnt* (pp. 1–24). London: Equality and Diversity Unit.

Eliot, P., & Roen, K. (1998). Transgenderism and the question of embodiment: Promising queer politics? *GLQ: Journal of Lesbian and Gay Studies, 4*(2), 231–261.

European Union Agency for Fundamental Rights (FRA). (2014). *EU LGBT survey*. Vienna: FRA.

FBI. (2014). *Hate crime statistics 2014: Victims*. Retrieved from https://ucr.fbi.gov/about-us/cjis/ucr/hate-crime/2014/topic-pages/victims_final.

FBI. (2015). *Criminal Justice Information Services (CJIS) Division Uniform Crime Reporting (UCR) program: Hate crime data collection guidelines and training manual*. Retrieved from https://ucr.fbi.gov/hate-crime-data-collection-guidelines-and-training-manual.pdf.

FBI. (n.d.). *Civil Rights: Matthew Shepard/James Byrd, Jr., Hate Crimes Prevention Act of 2009.* Retrieved from https://www.fbi.gov/about-us/investigate/civil rights/hate_crimes/shepard-byrd-act-brochure.

Fox, S. (1999). Damages awarded after transexual woman's death. *Polare, 44.*

Halberstam, J. (2003). The Brandon Teena archive. In R. J. Corber & S. Valocchi (Eds.), *Queer studies: An interdisciplinary reader* (pp. 159–169). Oxford: Blackwell.

Jamel, J. (2017) Transgender offenders within the prison estate: A comparative analysis of penal policy. In A. King, C. Santos, & I. Crowhurst (Eds.), *Sexualities Research: Critical Interjections, Diverse Methodologies and Practical Applications, 'Advances in Critical Diversities' series* (pp. 167–181). Abingdon: Routledge.

Kelley, P. (2009). *Filling in the blanks: Hate crime in London.* London.

Kenagy, G. P. (2005). Transgender health: Findings from two needs-assessments studies in Philadelphia. *Health and Social Work, 30*(1), 19–26.

Kenagy, G. P., & Bostwick, W. B. (2005). Health and social service needs of transgender people in Chicago. In W. Bockting & E. Avery (Eds.), *Transgender health and HIV prevention* (pp. 57–66). New York: Haworth Medical Press.

Kuehnle, K., & Sullivan, A. (2001). Patterns of anti-gay violence: An analysis of incident characteristics and victim reporting. *Journal of Interpersonal Violence, 16,* 928–943.

Lloyd, M. (2013). Heteronormativity and/as violence: The "sexing" of Gwen Araujo. *Hypatia, 28*(4), 818–834.

McDevitt, J., Farrell, A., Rousseau, D., & Wolff, R. (2013). Hate crimes: Characteristics of incidents, victims, and offenders. In R. C. Davis, A. J. Lurigio, & S. Herman (Eds.), *Victims of crime* (4th ed., pp. 107–132). London: Sage.

Moran, L. J., & Sharpe, A. N. (2004). Violence, identity and policing: The case of violence against transgender people. *Criminal Justice, 4*(4), 395–417.

Parsons, T., & Bales, R. F. (1956). *Family, socialization and interaction process.* London: Routledge and Kegan Paul.

Perry, B. (2003). Where do we go from here? Researching hate crime. *Internet Journal of Criminology,* 1–59.

Reed, B., Rhodes, S., Schofield, P., & Wylie, K. (2009). *Gender variance in the UK: Prevalence, incidence, growth and geographic distribution.* London: GIRES.

Rice, S. K., & Piquero, A. R. (2005). Perceptions of discrimination and justice in New York. *City Policing: An International Journal of Police Strategies & Management, 28*(1), 98–117.

Roen, K. (2001). Transgender theory and embodiment: The risk of racial marginalisation. *Journal of Gender Studies, 10*(3), 253–263.

Sandholtz, N., Langton, L., & Planty, M. (2013). *Hate crime victimization, 2003–2011*. Washington. Retrieved from http://www.bjs.gov/content/pub/pdf/hcv0311.pdf.

Schilt, K., & Westbrook, L. (2009). Doing gender, doing heteronormativity: Doing "gender normals", transgender people, and the social maintenance of heterosexuality. *Gender and Society, 23*(4), 440–464.

Serano, J. (2009). *Psychology, sexualization and trans-invalidations*. Paper presented at the 8th Annual Philadelphia Trans-Health Conference, Philadelphia. Retrieved from http://www.juliaserano.com/av/Serano-TransInvalidations.pdf.

Smith, K., Lader, D., Hoare, J., & Lau, I. (2012). *Hate crime, cyber security and the experience of crime among children: Findings from the 2010/11 British Crime Survey: Supplementary Volume 3 to Crime in England and Wales 2010/11*. London: Home Office.

Stotzer, R. L. (2009). Violence against transgender people: A review of United States data. *Aggression and Violent Behavior, 14,* 170–179.

Swiebel, J., & van der Veur, D. (2009). Hate crimes against lesbian, gay, bisexual and transgender persons and the policy response of international governmental organisations. *Netherlands Quarterly of Human Rights, 27*(4), 485–524.

Transgender Europe (TGEU). (2016). *TMM IDAHOT 2016 Update*. Retrieved from www.transrespect.org/en/trans-murder-monitoring/tmm-resources/.

Turner, L., Whittle, S., & Combs, R. (2009). *Transphobic hate crime in the EU*. Retrieved February 15, 2016, from http://www.ilga-europe.org/sites/default/files/transphobic_hate_crime_in_the_european_union_0.pdf.

United Nations Development Fund (UNDP). (2010). *Hijras/Transgender women in India: HIV, human rights and social exclusion*. New Delhi: Author.

Whittle, S., Turner, L., & Al-Alami, M. (2007). *Engendered penalties: Transgender and transsexual people's experiences of inequality and discrimination*. London: The Equalities Review.

Witten, T. M. (2003). Life-course analysis—The courage to search for something more: Middle adulthood issues in the transgender and intersex community. *Journal of Human Behavior in the Social Environment, 8*(2/3), 189–224.

Wolff, K. B., & Cokely, C. L. (2007). "To protect and serve?" An exploration of police conduct in relation to the gay, lesbian, bisexual, and transgender community. *Sexuality and Culture, 11,* 1–23.

Xavier, J. M. (2000). *The Washington, DC Transgender Needs Assessment Survey: Final Report for Phase 2: Tabulation of the survey questionnaires; Presentation of findings and analysis of the survey results; and recommendations.* Washington, DC: Administration for HIV/AIDS of the District of Columbia Government.

Yeung, P. (2016, July 28). Transphobic hate crimes rise 170% in five years. *The Independent.*

3

Legislation and the Protection of Trans People's Rights

Abstract In this chapter, the focus is on legislation which is pivotal with regard to the gradual process of promoting attitude change and facilitating policy-making decisions. The laws discussed for the purposes here relate to protected characteristics of individuals in relation to gender and sexual orientation. The national context: England, Scotland, Wales and Northern Ireland is considered regarding the progressiveness or lack of it in relation to the level of protection provided to trans people based on their gender and sexual orientation. These are also examined within the context of international laws in Ireland and other EU countries (including Bulgaria, Germany, Italy, Latvia and the Czech Republic), and America. In addition, the challenges resulting from the often close and symbiotic relationship between religious institutions and the State are also considered.

Keywords Gender identity · Legislation · National · International History · Religion · Morality

Historically, there have been strong links between the Church and State which have served to reinforce the gendered nature of legislation,

J. Jamel, *Transphobic Hate Crime*, Palgrave Hate Studies,
https://doi.org/10.1007/978-3-319-57879-8_3

heteronormativity, heteropatriarchy and the perception of a gender dichotomous society (see Halpern 1990; Weeks 1981 on law and homosexuality, for e.g.). Therefore, parallels can be drawn with regard to society's reluctance to accept same-sex relations as being normative together with their unwillingness to recognise the existence of multiple gender identities which is at odds with the religious and moral influences that reinforce the predominantly heteronormative laws in society. The underlying aim of which is to facilitate and ensure the procreation of the species. The influences of racism, colonialism, current religious and political dialogues are also central to understand why there is an aversion to accept multiple gender identities which persist globally. For a discussion of these factors in relation to Commonwealth countries, refer to the work of Lennox and Waites (2013), as it is beyond the scope of the current text.

These discussions also underscore the issues considered in Chap. 2 in relation to intersectionality. When discussing gender identity and the law, it is useful to also re-examine the term '*gender identity*'. For example, it is understood under the Yogyakarta Principles '…to refer to each person's deeply felt internal and individual experience of gender, which may or may not correspond with the sex assigned at birth, including the personal sense of the body (which may involve, if freely chosen, modification of bodily appearance or function by medical, surgical or other means) and other expressions of gender, including dress, speech and mannerisms' (The International Commission of Jurists and the International Service for Human Rights 2007, p. 8). An illustrative English case in relation to the complexity of gender identification is that of Corbett v Corbett (1970). This was a case where the petitioner wanted to dissolve his marriage to a trans woman (whom he knew to be transgender prior to marriage but now wanted to avoid inheritance issues by divorcing her) 14 days after its enactment. She had undergone gender confirmation surgery, but his wife April Ashley was still declared by the judge to be a natal male based on her male chromosomal sex, male gonadal sex, male genital sex and psychologically to be a transsexual which nullified the marriage as it could not be consummated. The historical importance of this example lies in the message being sent to society that gender is immutable irrespective as to whether someone has undergone gender confirmation surgery and regardless of their gender presentation and self-identification.

Although the focus here is predominantly on legislation in England and Wales, for comparative purposes, references are also made to Scotland, Northern Ireland and the Republic of Ireland. The protection trans people receive from gender bias crimes internationally under European Laws and federal legislation in America will also be discussed. Furthermore, countries in Europe and particular American states will also be highlighted that still do not have any hate crime legislation to target bias crimes based on transgender and gender nonconforming identities.

Hate Crime Legislation in England and Wales, Scotland and Northern Ireland

There are a number of legislative provisions such as the Police Reform Act 2002 which are supposed to protect trans people. This Act introduced new guidelines on dealing with complaints regarding police discrimination in relation to gender reassignment. Furthermore, since the Corbett v Corbett case, there have been fundamental and progressive changes in the law in England and Wales such as The Gender Recognition Act (GRA) 2004, Equality Act 2010 and the Legal Aid, Sentencing and Punishment of Offenders Act 2012 to target discrimination against trans and gender nonconforming individuals and the increasing recognition of their needs and rights in society.

The key legislation in England and Wales that has improved the protocols in order to protect the rights of transgender individuals is the GRA 2004. Underpinning some of those are Harry Benjamin's Standards of Care regarding the identification and treatment of gender dysphoria. However, these Standards of Care reinforce the gender binary with no allowance for other gender categories (Cole et al. 2000). This is irrespective of the extent of treatment undertaken, from hormone therapy to gender confirmation surgery, the purpose of which is to transition to the person's psychologically based gender. Thus, reinforcing the binary gender system within heterosexist society, however, there is no scope or provision for a third 'gender' which would accommodate bigender or agender individuals. Nevertheless, a positive aspect of this legislation is that it prevents trans individual's gender identity being disclosed to third parties without their consent which is of pivotal importance regarding their treatment by the police when reporting their criminal victimisation. Therefore, from the initial report at the front desk, or via the telephone through the Command Control Centre, or police being called to the scene; to the assignment of a specialist officer such as a Lesbian Gay Bisexual Transgender Liaison Officer (LGBT LO) or Hate Crime Specialist Officer; the case must be sensitively handled in accordance with the guidelines of the GRA 2004. The person must be referred to in accordance with how they present and if the officer is unsure how to address the person, they should ask them how they wish to be addressed and thus setting the tone of respect regarding the police encounter.

It was mentioned in Chap. 2 about the low reporting of transphobic hate crime, however, this does not automatically mean that there are fewer crimes; it may just be that there is a reluctance to report such incidents to the police. Trans or gender non-conforming people may have partners and families who are unaware of their preferred sexual orientation or gender identity. Thus, their fear is that by reporting the crime they risk being 'outed' through the criminal justice process. The ramifications of this may result in unemployment, becoming homeless and consequently a lowering of their socio-economic status despite the introduction of legislation to protect them. Legislation that aims to protect trans people such as Schedule 21 section 146 of the Criminal Justice Act 2003 amended by s.65(9) of the Legal Aid, Sentencing and Punishment of Offenders Act 2012 which made 'transgender' a protected characteristic. This legislation enabled enhanced sentencing for aggravated crimes motivated by hostility against trans individuals. For example, sentencing for murder offences aggravated by the person's transgender identity now starts at a 30-year tariff rather than the previous tariff of 15 years (CPS 2013). Sexual victimisation of trans people may also be a component of transphobic hate crime as discussed in Chap. 1. The fear of rape and experience of it by vaginaed men may differ from penile women. The motivation for rape in these cases is to re-affirm the gender binary. Prior to the GRA 2004 trans women would not have been protected from vaginal rape and trans men may have escaped prosecution for the perpetration of rape.

According to the GRA 2004 the following applies:

> Where an offender was a female at birth, but has since been legally acknowledged as a man by the application and grant of a Gender Recognition Certificate, he will have acquired the male gender at the time of the offence. In this case he is quite capable of committing the offence of rape (subject to all other considerations) and the offence will still be complete as per Section 3(a) … Conversely, if a victim was a male at birth but had acquired the female gender at the time of the offence, and is raped by a male, then the offence is similarly made out as per Section 3(b)… (ACPO 2005, p. 6).

Thus, the Sexual Offences Act 2003 now addresses the sexual victimisation of trans women and trans men on an equal basis of their non-transgender [this term is used by the author as an alternative to 'cisgender' as aforementioned due to possible discriminatory interpretations with regard to in-group/out-group usage (see Freeman as cited in Brydum 2015)] counterparts.

Prior to 2004, the law stated that sex was immutable and static. However, the GRA 2004 fundamentally changed this socially understood 'fact'. Under this Act the following criteria are applied: (i) one is over 18 and (ii) diagnosed with gender dysphoria where there is cognitive dissonance between the person's physical and psychological sex; (iii) provides evidence of having lived in their 'acquired gender' for a minimum of one year [i.e., undertaking a 'social gender role transition' previously known as 'Real Life Experience' (RLE)] and (iv) would live in their 'acquired gender' permanently. Once these criteria were met they could then apply for a Gender Recognition Certificate (GRC) to change their birth certificate and passport to their 'acquired gender'. This was a radical change in the law especially as a person did not have to undergo gender confirmation surgery to obtain a GRC. Nevertheless, the aforementioned provision of evidence, in the form of utility bills and other personal documents could prove to be quite a humiliating process. The key issue with this legislation is that it reinforces the gender binary as it does not allow for a 'third gender'. Also, historically, when individuals were diagnosed as suffering from gender identity disorder (GID), this pathologised them suggesting individuals were disordered. The Diagnostic Statistical Manual (DSM) V removed GID and now only gender dysphoria is referred to. The pressure felt by some trans people to undergo gender confirmation surgery in order to conform to socially ascribed gender norms could also be interpreted as society condoning violence against the transgender body to reassert the hegemonic gender binary. Therefore, if society was more gender inclusive with regard to multiple genders, then this may alleviate the pressure to conform to the gender dichotomy. The fact that one must agree to live as their acquired gender until death is in marked contrast to the gender flexibility permitted by indigenous societies discussed in Chap. 1. This Act reinforces gender norms discussed in Chap. 2 regarding socialised gender roles in society. It does not recognise a 'third gender' or gender queer identities. At the time of writing, the government is reviewing the GRA 2004 as it is now outdated. It is therefore considering ways in which changing one's gender legally may be made less intrusive, for example.

Secondary Victimisation

The Equality Act 2010 is important regarding the targeting of discrimination against trans people and the increasing recognition of their needs and rights in society. It is noteworthy here as institutional gender discrimination by healthcare professionals (see Witten 2003; Whittle et al. 2007) and inappropriate or insensitive police response can exacerbate experiences of trans and non-binary people regarding their transphobic victimisation (Antjoule 2016). The latter will be discussed in more detail in Chap. 5.

Victims' Rights

The Domestic Crime and Victims Act 2004 is the first law in England to specify 'victims' in the title, however, the law is 'toothless' with regard to its enforcement of victims' rights. Those who experience hate crime victimisation have the right to a range of entitlements with regard to advocacy, service referral and delivery in relation to justice agencies. If people who are in receipt of these services are dissatisfied, they may seek redress through the Parliamentary and Health Service Ombudsman. Nevertheless, the wording of the legislation is equivocal as victims are entitled to various services (see below) but do not automatically receive them. The Code of Practice for Victims of Crime established a right for those who report hate crime to be offered a referral to a specialist support service where locally available. In London, they may be referred to agencies such as GALOP (see Chap. 5 for a discussion of their organisation) or other relevant services. Otherwise, victims may be referred to more general organisations like Victim Support in areas lacking specialist services. GALOP in their recent report recommends victims' rights be made enforceable by law, as evidenced in Scottish legislation under the Victims' Rights Regulations 2015 (Antjoule 2016).

Scotland

In Scotland, legislation targeting hate crime was passed in 2009 in the form of the Offences (Aggravation by Prejudice) Scotland Act 2009. Although this legislation relates to both sexual orientation and transgender identity, the focus here will be on all aspects of this law in relation to the latter characteristic only. In this Act, references to 'transgender identity' encompass transvestism, transsexualism, intersexuality or someone who has changed gender via the GRA 2004 but is also inclusive of any non-binary genders (http://www.legislation.gov.uk/asp/2009/8/section/2) which is quite progressive. An offence that is aggravated by prejudice relating to transgender identity proved at the time of the offence being committed, or immediately before/after the incident where the offender's motivation (wholly or partly) for their acts towards the victim is indicative of malice and ill-will relating to the person's transgender identity or perceived identity can result in enhanced sentencing, this is discussed below.

It is also immaterial if the offender's actions are motivated by any additional factors. Evidence from a single source is sufficient to prove the offence is aggravated by prejudice relating to transgender identity. The court must also state on the conviction that the offence is aggravated by prejudice in relation to the victim's transgender identity and this aspect must also be recorded, this factor must then be taken into account when sentencing (http://www.legislation.gov.uk/asp/2009/8/section/2). The number of transphobic crimes charged was 21 for the period 2014–2015 which was a little lower than the 2012–2013 when it was 25 (Crown Office and Procurator Fiscal Service 2015). In the 2015–2016 period, there were 30 transphobic crimes charged illustrating a slight increase, and in 77% of those charges court proceedings were commenced (Crown Office and Procurator Fiscal Service 2016). Unfortunately, the outcomes of these cases were not published. For the period 2016–17, 40 charges were reported with an aggravation on prejudice pertaining to transgender identity that is 10 more than the 2015–2016 period. Furthermore court proceeding were commenced in 80% of the charges which is again an improvement on the previous year. Next, the legal situation regarding transphobic hate crime in Northern Ireland is explored.

Northern Ireland

In Northern Ireland, Part 3 of the Public Order NI Order 1987 criminalises 'acts intended or likely to stir up hatred or arouse fear and specifically relates to the use of '…threatening, abusive or insulting words or behaviour and the display of written material which is threatening, abusive or insulting…' (http://www.legislation.gov.uk/nisi/1987/463/article/9) and targets hate crime on the basis of religious belief, colour, race, nationality (including citizenship) or ethnic or national origins. In 2004, the Criminal Justice Act (No. 2) Northern Ireland Order 2004 was passed which extended the definition of hate crime to incidents motivated by hatred against individuals because of their sexual orientation or disability. In section 2 of this Act it also enabled an increase in sentence if there was hostility against the victim who possessed or was perceived to possess any of the aforementioned characteristics, whereby this was then understood as an aggravating factor in the crime committed (The Stationery Office 2004). At the time of writing, the legal situation in Northern Ireland regarding transphobic hate crime is that there is no specific legal protection for trans people against this type of hate crime. It should also be noted that there are no laws preventing the stirring up of hatred against trans people in England, Wales and Northern Ireland (Antjoule 2016).

The Republic of Ireland

At the time of writing, the Republic of Ireland does not have explicit hate crime legislation. The reasons given for this lack of provision are (1) hate speech law as it stands is considered to prohibit incitement to hatred offences; (2) current legislation in relation to criminal offences is considered appropriate to address hate crime; (3) there is judicial discretion to treat any 'hate factor' as an aggravating factor and thus sentences may be enhanced in this regard where a hate element is substantiated (Haynes et al. 2015). Nonetheless, the Criminal Law (Hate Crime) Amendment Bill 2015 has yet to be passed despite mounting national pressure from the LGBT community that this should be one of the main priorities. In addition to addressing institutional and social discriminations experienced daily, as well as reviewing and developing more comprehensive legislation to resolve the limitations of the current provision. It is also important to explore the extent of the legal protection of trans people from hate crime in other European countries, as this would impact on the mobility of trans people in Europe.

Hate Crime Legislation in EU Countries

In Table 1 below, the distinct lack of provision in Bulgaria, the Czech Republic, Germany, Italy and Latvia is evidenced. However, the Directive 2012/29/EU established minimum standards on the rights, support and protection of victims of crime which were adopted on 25 October 2012 and passed into law on 15 November 2012 with all EU member states required to incorporate this legislation into their national laws by 15 November 2015 (European Commission 2015). This law gave improved protection to victims of specific crimes such as hate crime. Nevertheless, it is not clear how the incorporation of this legal instrument across all EU

Table 1 The lack of legal protection against homophobic and transphobic hate crimes in select EU countries is outlined

Bulgaria	Criminal Code Articles 162, 163 and 165	Violence and group violence against a person or property on grounds including race, religion, nationality or political convictions are stand-alone offences
Czech Republic	Criminal Code Articles 219, 221, 222 and 257	For some offences (including murder, physical assault, criminal damage) motives relating to the race, ethnicity or political belief of the victim(s) can be considered as aggravating circumstances when sentencing
	Criminal Code Article 196	Violence motivated to a large extent by the political conviction, nationality, race, religion or belief of the victim is a standalone offence
Germany	Criminal Code	No provision on hate crime
	Police criminal registration system	Hate crime is a sub-category of 'politically motivated crimes'. There are two types of hate crime: xenophobic and anti-Semitic
Italy	Law no 654 of 13 October 1975 (subsequently amended in 1989, 1993 and 2006)	Violence, or inciting violence, on the grounds of race, ethnic origin, nationality or religion, is a stand-alone offence. Perpetrating any other crime on the grounds of race, ethnic origin, nationality or religion is an aggravating circumstance
Latvia	Criminal Code Section 48	Perpetrating a crime with a racist motive is an aggravating circumstance
Non-EU		Gaps exist in legislation including in neighbouring states such as Ukraine and Moldova and in acceding and candidate states such as Turkey, FYROM (Macedonia) and Montenegro

This table is extracted from Amnesty International (2013), p. 6

member state's respective national legislation will be ensured or any sanctions for non-compliance. Thus, the effectiveness and utility of this law remains to be seen but it is a progressive step forward regarding the raising of awareness of the seriousness with which hate crimes will be treated. Next, the diversity regarding the protection of trans people from transphobic hate crime under American legislation is explored.

United States of America

Hate crime legislation and related policies that have identified a specific type or subset of criminality are quite recent in the USA as seen below. For example, a populist definition of hate crime was not established until the 1970s. Furthermore, authors have noted that determining the punishment to address hate speech, for example, is considered problematic by some regarding the possible contravention of the First Amendment Protection which protects freedom of speech and the legal debate around this matter continues (McDevitt et al. 2013).

Hate crimes began to be recognised under the law in the USA with the passing of the Hate Crime Statistics Act in 1990, followed by an amended version whereby hate crimes against disabled people were included in the Violent Crime Control and Law Enforcement Act 1994. Next, the Church Arson Prevention Act 1996 established the collection of hate crime statistics as permanent within the Uniform Crime Reports Program (Sandholtz et al. 2013). A pivotal piece of legislation in the USA was that of the Hate Crime Sentencing Enhancement Act 1994. The sentencing penalties were thus able to be increased in federal cases as a result of this Act—where the evidence confirms that the victim was targeted because of their ethnicity, religion, gender, race, disability or sexual orientation. The Hate Crimes Prevention Act 1998 further expanded the federal jurisdiction; this enabled the investigation and prosecution of crimes motivated by hate, while also augmenting the protection and contextual safeguards (McDevitt et al. 2013). Moreover, the Matthew Shepard and James Byrd, Jr. Hate Crimes Prevention Act (HCPA) 2009 was another key and long awaited development as it finally closed a legal loophole in federal law. This loophole had previously only permitted federal involvement in the investigation and prosecution of hate crime cases only within the context of when the victim targeted was undertaking a federal duty such as jury service. The HCPA 2009 also increased federal protection in relation to hate crimes motivated by actual or perceived (this is an important distinction) characteristic or identity with regard to non-specific victims being targeted. Instead, it is their representation of a particular group which is key, for example, sexual orientation, gender, gender identity and disability. In addition, another important element of the HCPA was that it amended the Hate Crime Sentencing Enhancement Act so that the FBI was mandated to collate hate crime data on gender, gender identity and juveniles commission of hate crimes (McDevitt et al. 2013). This law also allowed federal jurisdiction to supersede state law where it was inadequate or local authorities were reluctant to investigate cases enabling the FBI to investigate and prosecute such crimes (ADL 2016). It is noteworthy that in 2011 only 13 states provided protection for those individuals targeted because of their gender identity (McDevitt et al. 2013) suggesting more progress in this regard has yet to be made.

Nonetheless, as detailed below, the recognition of hate crimes based on gender bias took a significantly longer time to be legally addressed. On occasion, a particular type of defence was often attempted to be used in relation to more extreme types of transphobic hate crimes such as homicides. This type of defence is described as a 'trans panic defence' (see the previously discussed Araujo case). In 2006, in California the then-Governor Arnold Schwarzenegger signed into law the '*Gwen Araujo Justice for Victims Act*, which stated that the use of societal bias, including so-called 'panic strategies', to influence the proceedings of a criminal trial is not permitted' (Adams 2012). This was an important step in highlighting that the targeting of trans people on the basis of their gender identity or perceived gender identity is unacceptable in society.

In 2009, there was a change in federal hate crimes law which was pivotal in facilitating the prosecution of violent acts and attempted violence directed at gay, lesbian and transgender individuals. The new law was the aforementioned Matthew Shepard and James Byrd, Jr., Hate Crimes Prevention Act which provided interjurisdictional funding to investigate, prosecute and help prevent hate crime (FBI, n.d.). The current situation in the USA at the time of writing is that only five states have no legal protection for trans people from hate crimes; these are Arkansas, Georgia, Indiana, South Carolina and Wyoming. However, there is a variation in the list of protected classes. For example, the following 15 states have hate crime legislation but it does not address gender identity or sexual orientation: Alabama, Alaska, Idaho, Michigan, Mississippi, Montana, North Carolina, North Dakota, Ohio, Oklahoma, Pennsylvania, South Dakota, Utah, Virginia and West Virginia (http://www.hrc.org/state_maps). Thus, there is still some progress to be made in these states regarding the protection of trans people's rights and the taking of trans phobic hate crime seriously. Furthermore, the aforementioned lack of hate crime legislation protecting trans people thus restricts their freedom of movement on an interstate basis. Finally, despite oppostion to its usage, the controversial trans panic defence was again employed quite recently by Joseph Scott Pemberton in the Jennifer Laude case. In October 2014, she was allegedly killed by Pemberton in the Philippines. She had performed oral intercourse on him, after which he found out that she possessed male genitalia which resulted in him panicking and flying into a rage and choking her (Talusan 2015). The rage was motivated by the perceived gender deception that she had engaged in resulting in extreme violence being perpetrated against her. The extreme level of violence described here is also referred to in Chap. 4.

This chapter has provided insight into the varied legislation across a number of territories from England and Wales to Northern Ireland, Scotland, Europe and the USA. It has also demonstrated that there is work to be done across these territories to tackle the issue of transphobic hate crime. Bettcher (2007) makes a very valid point with regard to the legislative changes discussed above, such as the prohibition of the 'trans panic defence', that it is only one of the many approaches required to address this crime. The institutional discrimination within the criminal justice system experienced by transgender ethnic minority victims also needs to be considered when examining the criminal justice response to transgender victims of hate crime. This is one of the many factors referred to in the next chapter which addresses the victim–offender relationship and its many facets from victim and offender demographics to the phenomenology of transphobic hate crimes and the motivation of offenders who perpetrate these crimes.

References

ACPO (2005). *The Gender Recognition Act 2004: Guidance for police officers and staff.* London, ACPO: 1–19.

Adams, N. (2012). *Gwen Araujo murdered ten years ago today*. Retrieved Feb 16, 2016, from http://www.glaad.org/blog/gwen-araujo-murdered-ten-years-ago-today.

Amnesty International. (2013). *Because of who I am: Homophobia, transphobia and hate crimes in Europe*. Retrieved from https://www.amnesty.at/de/view/files/download/showDownload/?tool=12&feld=download&sprach_connect=304.

Anti-Defamation League (ADL). (2016). *Combating hate: Hate crimes law: ADL: Hate crimes information for law enforcement: Definition of hate crime.* Retrieved from http://www.adl.org/combating-hate/hate-crimes-law/c/hate-crimes-information-for-law-enforcement.html#.V80nIJgrLIV.

Antjoule, N. (2016). *The hate crime report: Homophobia, biphobia and transphobia in the UK.* London. Retrieved from http://www.galop.org.uk/wp-content/uploads/2016/10/The-Hate-Crime-Report-2016.pdf.

Bettcher, T. M. (2007). Evil deceivers and make-believers: On transphobic violence and the politics of illusion. *Hypatia, 22*(3), 43–65.

Brydum, S. (2015, July 31). *The true meaning of the word 'cisgender': It's not complicated: Cisgender is the opposite of transgender. The Advocate*, Retrieved from https://www.advocate.com/transgender/2015/07/31/true-meaning-word-cisgender.

Cole, S. S., Denny, D., Eyler, A. E., & Samons, S. L. (2000). Issues of transgender. In L. Szuchman & F. Muscarella (Eds.), *Psychological perspectives on human sexuality* (pp. 149–195). New York: Wiley.

Corbett v Corbett (1970).

CPS (2013). *Sentencing: Procedure in cases to which section 146 CJA 2003 applies*. Retrieved Feb 29, 2016, from http://www.cps.gov.uk/legal/h_to_k/homophobic_and_transphobic_hate_crime/.

Crown Office and Procurator Fiscal. (2015). *Hate crime in Scotland in 2014–15.* Edinburgh: Author.

Crown Office and Procurator Fiscal Service. (2016). *Hate crime in Scotland in 2015–16.* Edinburgh: Author.

European Commission. (2015). *Justice: Building a European area of justice: Victims.* Retrieved from http://ec.europa.eu/justice/criminal/victims/index_en.htm.

FBI. (n.d.). *Civil Rights: Matthew Shepard/James Byrd, Jr., Hate Crimes Prevention Act of 2009.* Retrieved from https://www.fbi.gov/about-us/investigate/civilrights/hate_crimes/shepard-byrd-actbrochure.

Halpern, D. M. (1990). *One hundred years of homosexuality.* New York: Routledge.

Haynes, A., Schweppe, J., & Carr, J. (2015). *Out of the shadows: Legislating for hate crime in Ireland.* Limerick: University of Limerick.

Lennox, C., & Waites, M. (2013). Human rights, sexual orientation and gender identity in the commonwealth: From history and law to developing activism and transnational dialogues. In C. Lennox & M. Waites (Eds.), *Human rights, sexual orientation and gender identity in the commonwealth* (pp. 1–59). London: Human Rights Consortium, Institute of Commonwealth Studies.

McDevitt, J., Farrell, A., Rousseau, D., & Wolff, R. (2013). Hate crimes: Characteristics of incidents, victims, and offenders. In R. C. Davis, A. J. Lurigio, & S. Herman (Eds.), *Victims of crime* (4th ed., pp. 107–132). London: Sage.

Sandholtz, N., Langton, L., & Planty, M. (2013). *Hate crime victimization, 2003–2011.* Washington. Retrieved from http://www.bjs.gov/content/pub/pdf/hcv0311.pdf.

Talusan, M. (2015). Jennifer Laude's death would've caused an outcry—If she wasn't transgender. *The Guardian.* Retrieved from https://www.theguardian.com/commentisfree/2015/jul/28/jennifer-laude-death-transgender-philippines.

The Stationery Office (2004). *Explanatory notes to Gender Recognition Act 2004 Chapter 7,* pp. 1–13. London: Author.

The International Commission of Jurists and the International Service for Human Rights. (2007). *The Yogyakarta principles: Principles on the application of international human rights law in relation to sexual orientation and gender identity.* Retrieved from http://www.yogyakartaprinciples.org.

Weeks, J. (1981). Inverts, perverts, and Mary-Annes: Male prostitution and the regulation of homosexuality in England in the nineteenth and twentieth centuries. *Journal of Homosexuality, 6*(1/2), 113–134.

Whittle, S., Turner, L., & Al-Alami, M. (2007). *Engendered penalties: Transgender and transsexual people's experiences of inequality and discrimination.* London: The Equalities Review.

Witten, T. M. (2003). Life-course analysis—The courage to search for something more: Middle adulthood issues in the transgender and intersex community. *Journal of Human Behavior in the Social Environment, 8*(2/3), 189–224.

4
The Victim–Offender Relationship in Transphobic Hate Crime

Abstract The victim–offender relationship is important to discern from the crime scene actions in order to identify whether they were known to the victim or not and their motivations for the attack. This is to assist in the identification of the offender(s) in order to achieve justice for the victim. However, homicides or physical and sexual acts of violence are not always recorded as transphobic or motivated by transgender hate crime bias. There has thus far been very limited research conducted on hate crime offenders. Nevertheless, a typology of hate crime has been developed and will be discussed here. In addition, the characteristics of the offenders and victims are also examined together with the police response to victims to further contextualise the nature of transphobic crime.

Keywords Victim · Offender · Motivation · Offender typology · Police response · Transphobic hate crime

A hate crime is a criminal act which targets a person or property due to the perpetrator's perception of the victim as being of a particular race, religion, ethnicity, national origin, sexual orientation, disability or gender

J. Jamel, *Transphobic Hate Crime*, Palgrave Hate Studies,
https://doi.org/10.1007/978-3-319-57879-8_4

(ADL 2016). It is therefore important to note that it is not a specific victim being targeted but who they represent with regard to their perceived or real membership of a particular group, victims are understood by the perpetrators as being interchangeable in this regard. Thus, the person has not been identified for victimisation because of something they have done and hence are innocent of any wrongdoing. Also, it is noteworthy that hate crimes more often involve multiple offenders, which result in extreme cruelty being perpetrated during the attack (McDevitt et al. 2013).

Transphobic hate crime suggests that it is motivated by the offender's fear of trans people based solely on their physical appearance, which indicates that there is an irrational element to this crime. Alternatively, this crime could be conceptualised as a focused attack against a gender minority who as a group threaten the dichotomous gender hierarchy within a patriarchal society that is legitimated by a hegemonic social order. The emotive elements of fear and hatred can inform a perpetrator's motivation to commit a transphobic hate crime. This criminal act not only targets an individual, but also sends a warning message to the wider trans community. There are many debates regarding the victim–offender relationship as to whether the perpetrator is known to the victim or is a stranger. The dynamics of this relationship will be analysed throughout the course of this chapter. If the victim is known to the offender, then this can increase the trauma of the experience particularly if they had been in a relationship with their attacker. Another factor which can increase the distress of the victim is if the perpetrator abuses their position of trust and authority such as those offenders who are law enforcement officers. The FBI statistics classify crimes as either hate or bias crimes based on the extreme nature and brutality of these crimes which exceeds an instrumental purpose in subduing the victim (McDevitt et al. 2013). Thus, the relentless and excessive violent physical assaults represent an *overkill* element as a consequence of the hate crime bias characteristic of this kind of homicide (see Kelley and Gruenewald 2015). This element of certain homicides is where there is a prolonged level of violence in excess of that needed to kill the victim. The extreme types of hate crime described above are at one end of the spectrum with the publically perceived minor types such as verbal and psychological violence being at the other end. However, this is not to say that the latter types of violence may not debilitate and be impactful on the recipients, so these volume hate crime acts shall also be examined. These 'minor' acts of transphobic hate crime are often neglected in favour of research focusing on physical and sexual violence and homicides. The aim here is to take a more holistic view examining transphobic hate crime acts, the perpetrators, victims and locations, all of which can impact on the ability and willingness of the victim to report, as well as exacerbating the potential trauma of their victimisation experience. Furthermore, the qualitatively different reaction to hate crime offenders who are perceived as morally repugnant due to the features of these crimes is also discussed. For example, hate crime offenders were considered more culpable than perpetrators of non-hate crimes (Rayburn et al. 2003). Therefore, in this chapter, the debates within the literature as to the nature of the victim-offender relationship will be explored together with the offender(s)' motivation and characteristics, such as gender, age and ethnicity.

Trans-identified survivors of hate crime violence accounted for 18% of all survivors in 2011 which is an increase of 2% from 2010 figures (see NCAVP 2012). To examine hate crime perpetrators' motivation, McDevitt et al.'s (2002) typology will be adapted for use regarding transphobic hate crime offenders, as originally their typology was developed in relation to hate crime offenders in general. Crime types will be explored in relation to contact and non-contact offenders. Also, the issues around 'gender deception' which is an oft-cited reason for transphobic violence in relation to this type of crime as highlighted in Chap. 3. The difference in vulnerability particularly in relation to trans men and women will also be explored as much of the research focuses on the latter population (Lombardi et al. 2001; Stotzer 2009, 2014). The intersectionality of victims also influences their vulnerability; this has been discussed earlier. However, in this chapter it will be considered in relation to the increased conspicuousness of these individuals and hostility from within their own ethnic community which exacerbates the trauma of victimisation. The gender of offenders will also be examined by considering the male perpetrators of transphobic violence and the passive aggressive violence used by females when outing a trans male colleague at work. The spectrum of violence thus ranges from the excessive violence of transphobic homicides to non-contact verbal violence or aggression.

The Victim–Offender Relationship

The victim–offender relationship was found to be similar to that of the perpetrators of sexual violence, i.e. that of acquaintance (Kelley 2009; Kuehnle and Sullivan 2003; Xavier et al. 2007). Research suggests that acquaintances composed the majority of perpetrators of sexual violence (48%), strangers (26%), father or step-father (16%), former spouse or partner (12%) or brother or sister (12%). Perpetrators of transphobic violence may include lovers, family members, friends, acquaintances and strangers met in streets or bars (Xavier et al. 2007). Although, Reback's (2001) study suggested that the perpetration of physical violence (involving direct physical contact) was in the main committed by strangers was (37%) and to a lesser extent, police (14%), parents (9%), siblings (4%), other relatives (3%) and friends (3%). However, there are few studies that focus on law enforcement officials who perpetrate transphobic hate crime (Wolff and Cokely 2007). In contrast, a more recent study by the NCAVP (2012) found that 'other known' offenders were the largest category of the offender (23%) although it is not clear who this group consisted of and must have been quite diverse if none of the stated categories captured the identity of these known offenders. The other categories of known offender were as follows: landlord/tenant/neighbour (20%); acquaintance/friend (18%); employer/co-worker; relative/family, and police were respectively (9%); service provider, and lover/partner were each (4%); ex-lover/partner (3%); roommate (1%); and 'other law enforcement (e.g. FBI, ICE)' and 'other first responder' (e.g. EMT, Court Personnel) (0%) respectively. Thus, considering that the offender is more likely to be known to the survivor, then it is not surprising that the location of transphobic attacks where information was available was private residences (18%) (NCAVP 2012). Thus, as can be seen from the above figures, the importance of education and raising awareness of hate violence against LGBTQ people but particularly trans people cannot be over-emphasised. This is also highlighted by Grant et al. (2011) in their study which examines hate crime violence within the employment sector, whereby discrimination and hate violence can result in trans and gender non-conforming people losing their job (over 25%), 19% experienced homelessness at some point and were four times more likely to be subject to extreme poverty at some point in their lives. According to respondents, unknown offenders composed 72% (which has decreased by 4% since 2010), who in the main were strangers to survivors, and other offenders accounted for 15%. There was also a noticeable decrease in unknown police offenders from 17% in 2010 to 8% in 2011, the remainder of the unknown offender dataset was composed of other law enforcement and first responders resulting in less than 3%.

Motivation

TENI (2014) in their Irish study suggest that there were multiple motivations identified by respondents which were gender expression (72%), gender identity (78%) and sexual orientation (75%). There is a scarcity of information in the available British literature regarding the perpetrators of this type of hate crime, with the majority of research on perpetrators being conducted in the USA (see McDevitt et al. 2002, 2013). In this research, they expanded upon their original typology of offender motivations for the commission of hate crime, consisting of (i) thrill (those who commit offences for the excitement or thrill), (ii) defensive (those who are defending their territory) and (iii) mission (self-appointed mission to eliminate those defined as lesser individuals or deviant) to also include retaliatory motivation (retaliation against the victim for a real or perceived slight). '…[T]he FBI has identified as an indicator of hate or bias crimes the tendency toward brutality exceeding the force necessary to subdue a victim. Furthermore, hate crimes are generally perpetrated by strangers in acts that can often appear to be random, senseless, or irrational' (McDevitt et al. 2013, p. 123).

Participants in Xavier et al.'s (2005) American study suggested that in 35% of cases the motivation was transphobia. As transgenderism challenges what are considered heteronormative gender schemas, it has been found that non-transgender men and women have a stronger reaction to trans individuals who transition to the 'opposite gender' but are still considered to be the same sex (Schilt and Westbrook 2009). Anderson (2008) draws parallels between what he describes as the 'one-time rule of homosexuality' (this is the same as the 'one-act rule of homosexuality' the only difference being the nomenclature) and the perception that if there was even a hint of Black ethnic origins in a person's background, they were deemed as being Black by the dominant White majority. Therefore, '…one same-sex sexual experience is equated with a homosexual orientation in masculine peer culture, ruling out the possibility of men engaging in recreational same-sex sexual acts without being homosexualized by their behaviour' (Anderson 2005a as cited in Anderson 2008 p. 105). If the 'one-act rule' is applied to the perpetration of sexual violence or in more extreme cases sexual homicide, the motivation could stem from this self-identification of possible latent homosexual tendencies resulting in cognitive dissonance regarding their sexual orientation which may only be alleviated by the retributive sexual and physical violence directed at the victim. This type of violent reaction by the offender has parallels with Groth's (1979) Conflict and Counteraction rapist, whereby the rapist has latent homosexual tendencies which are projected onto the male victim and through the act of rape the offender experiences a cathartic release from these internal conflicting sexual tensions. The use of such violence by males is condoned through its expression of masculinity and its reinforcement, whereas females' expression of femininity does not permit the same access to violence to repair the gender chasm. It is either negotiated and accepted or responded to in a passive aggressive manner through the disclosure of the man's transgender status or their natal female gender. Accordingly, a key aspect of transphobic violence is the threat to heteronormativity and construction of one's self-identity as reflected through the perception of others, and belief in the 'one-act rule of homosexuality'. Thus, in order to reaffirm one's heterosexuality, one must devalue and ridicule all gender and sexual deviations from socialised norms (see Hennen 2008; Pascoe 2007). Hence, this challenge to heteronormativity must be addressed in the perpetrator's view, through retaliation which may extend beyond the person inflicting the hurt in that instant; to historical experiences of personal injury. This occurs simultaneously with their perception of enforcing informal justice and correcting past wrongdoings, this process is suggested as underlying '…the offender's conscious cognition' (Iganski and Levin 2015, p. 55). Thus, the perpetration of hate crime for these offenders who have limited avenues for their expression of stress or upset, instead may channel these feelings into anger and violence at a conscious or unconscious level through which they obtain and maintain the respect of their peers and a sense of self-worth and dignity. In addition, these individuals because of their emotional sensitivity will be '… hyper-sensitive to infringements, transgressions, or disrespect. Once their sense of self is challenged, violence might be their only resource for rebuilding and protecting it' (Iganski and Levin 2015, p. 56).

An allegation frequently aimed at trans people by offenders as a defence or justification for their perpetration of transphobic hate crime is that they were deceived by the trans person not declaring their transgender status resulting in a gender deception. Nevertheless, there are differing attitudes to disclosure of their transgender status amongst trans people as some individuals may initially disclose their transgender status whereas other people no longer see themselves as transgender having transitioned and are therefore living authentically as their true self, either as a man or a woman. Thus, it is not perceived to be deceiving others about their gender or presenting themselves disguised as the opposite gender. By framing trans people in this way, it is suggested that they are performing their gender similar to a cross-dresser rather than living as their authentic selves. This allegation of trans people as being 'fraudulent', 'fakes' or 'evil deceivers' allows offenders to engage in victim blaming, whereby the victim has played a role in their own victimisation by precipitating the crime against them. This approach attempts to lay claim to the 'trans panic' defence which is a variation of the 'gay panic' defence used in the Matthew Shepard Case, this is particularly used to defend the offender's physical and/or sexual violence or even perpetration of homicide when they have been in an intimate relationship with the trans person (see Bettcher 2007 for a detailed discussion of the Gwen Araujo case and the defendant's use of a 'trans panic' defence). It is noteworthy here that in 49 out of 50 US states the 'gay and trans panic defences' may be used (Kemnitz 2014). However, in 2015, California became the first state to ban this type of defence in their AB-2501 revision of the Section 1 F1 and F2 Voluntary Manslaughter legislation which states that the defendant may not even attempt to convince a jury that the victim's gender and/or sexual orientation may be used as grounds for justifiable homicide. If the trans panic defence is deconstructed the concept of 'gender deception' must also be challenged. Otherwise the underlying assumption is that the defendant's interpretation of the victim's gender identity is privileged over the victim's own self-identified gender presentation in a heteronormative hierarchical framing of the victim–offender relationship. The underlying notion being that genitalia or one's sexual anatomy are the only signifiers of one's gender presentation irrespective of one's gender identity which is rejected by trans and gender non-conforming people. Gender confirmation surgery, the desire to access it and the ability to afford it has thus resulted in conflicting powerful and political debates.

Grant et al. (2011) suggests that not all trans people desire gender confirmation surgery, nevertheless their report stated that the majority of those surveyed did desire surgical interventions but are unable to afford it. The notion that trans or non-binary people should disclose their personal history to others from the outset is not expected of the non-transgender community. If it is not acceptable for strangers to ask non-transgender people about their genitalia, why is it considered acceptable to ask trans people that question? When the 'sexual truth' is exposed, then the transphobic offender justifies their violence as 'identity reinforcement' such as the raping of Brandon Teena reinforcing sexual essentialism (Bettcher 2007). When deconstructing such transphobic violence, the further complexity of the nature of this violence is explicit, and that is the exacerbating influence of homophobia and the 'one-act rule' of homosexuality which appears to destabilise the male offender's sense of his own sexual orientation and gender identity that has been constrained by hegemonic and heterosexist notions of masculinity and maleness. Next, types of transphobic hate crime are discussed regarding the variance in severity as well as examining the demographics of offenders engaged in this form of criminal behaviour.

Types of Transphobic Hate Crime Acts

Transphobic hate crime acts can range from non-contact to contact offences. Examples of non-contact offences include verbal violence ranging from epithets or taunts (shouted in the street or other public places) to psychological violence from academic theorists (see Raymond 1996). Raymond refers to Male-to-Female (MTF) or trans women as 'Gender Terrorists' asserting this is yet another form of oppression and sexism by males trying to exert power and control over female physical and sexual characteristics. Thus, trans women she alleges are usurping female identities and misrepresenting their biological selves, the result is overt psychological and verbal violence by labelling trans women as 'rapists' of natal women's bodies and their commodification of these bodies. There is also the transphobic verbal violence experienced online, whereby a recent study stated that 44% of the transgender respondents had experienced hate-motivated abuse (see Antjoule 2016).

Contact offenders' perpetration of physical and sexual violence, the severity of which can result in homicides due to the excessive nature of this violence and its emotion. This is resultant from the perceived threat to the perpetrators' own gender identity, binary gender and sexual orientation norms which are destabilised due to the conceptual challenge that non-binary individuals present.

There is also a difference with regard to locations of transphobic violence, as according to Kuehnle and Sullivan's (2001) study of the ten transgender victims who reported physical violence being perpetrated against them to a social service agency. Half stated they were victimised in a private residence, whereas 20% of crimes occurred on public transportation, 20% occurred in public accommodation and 10% in a public or an outdoor space. It is also important to note here that spatial awareness and perceived safe spaces prior to transition for a trans female may be perceived to be the same post-transition. For example, the inherent right of movement bestowed through hegemonic masculinity to walk around late at night in spaces females may perceive to be unsafe. This is reminiscent of theoretical perspectives espoused by victimologists such as Hindelang et al. (1978) in their lifestyle theory which discusses factors which increase one's likelihood of victimisation based on lifestyle, the areas they frequent, who they associate with, the motivation of potential offenders (to use force or stealth to achieve their desired aim) who cross paths with a potential victim where there is an absence of a capable guardian. The consequence of which for trans females is it may result in their being labelled a 'bad victim' (Moran and Sharpe 2004) for engaging in risky behaviour regarding their lifestyle and hence their legitimacy of victimhood is denied. This is particularly concerning in relation to transphobic victimisation and may further exacerbate the victim's traumatic experience. Hence, this issue needs to be addressed when responding to this type of crime and other violent crimes perpetrated against trans women. For trans men, a reversal of access rights may occur, in that places they once deemed unsafe prior to transition may now be considered safe spaces, as they now have the 'right' of masculine privilege to access such spaces with impunity irrespective of the time. Nevertheless, their willingness to do so may still be limited as a result of the legacy of their historical feminine experience. This particular gender difference with regard to gendered spatial awareness may therefore influence the likelihood of victimisation and inform the difference between trans female and trans male criminal victimisation and particularly transphobic victimisation. Next, the characteristics of the perpetrators of this type of crime are discussed.

Perpetrator Age

The most common age range was 19–29 where the age of the offender was known (NCAVP 2012). Thus, suggesting that this is the age at which awareness particularly needs to be raised through education programmes and the development of prevention strategies. It is also suggested that curricula at schools and universities also address LGBTQ violence and the consequences this violence can have on individuals' lifestyles and feelings of safety when engaging in everyday activities.

Perpetrator Gender Identity and Ethnicity

FORGE (2005 as cited in Stotzer 2009) found that the gender of the offenders was male (90%), female (30%) and transgender (12%) (the total does not add to 100% because assaults may have been by male offenders in one incident and a female in another, etc.). The gender of perpetrators of hate crime is predominantly young non-transgender males, with non-transgender females composing the minority of offenders (NCAVP 2012; Wolff and Cokely 2007). The ethnicity of hate crime offenders in recent research is configured as follows: according to a recent American study, 51% White, 24% Black, 19% Latino, 2% Indigenous/First People, 2% Asian/Pacific Islanders with Arab and Middle Eastern Offenders consisting of 3% (NCAVP 2012). There was an increase (+9%) in 2011 of White offenders and decrease (−11%) in Black offenders since 2010, but it is suggested that these variations were due to more accurate recording practices being used.

Number of Offenders

According to the NCAVP (2012) research, most victims reported a single offender while 20% reported two to five offenders with 1% reporting a larger group of six to nine or 'less than ten' offenders. It is suggested that hate crimes more than other types of crimes are perpetrated more frequently in groups with multiple offenders (McDevitt et al. 2002). The impact of this group violence is particularly exacerbated when targeting LGBTQ individuals as not only are there the usual group dynamics of the diffusion of responsibility (Darley and Latanè 1968), and peer reinforcement which encourages more severe violence, in this case to reassert heteronormative binary gender and sexual orientation norms. This type of violence may also be further aggravated by religious and moral ideologies which incite a collective rage or hate towards the survivor's identity which is considered to deviate from socially ascribed gender and sexual orientation norms.

Survivor Gender Identity and Ethnicity

There are a disproportionate number of trans women and ethnic minority trans people being murdered. For example, of the 30 hate murders committed, 87% of the total number of victims were from ethnic minority communities whereas 50% of the total sample were ethnic minority individuals from the LGBTQ community. It was also noted that 40% of the total number of homicide victims were trans women and 50% were non-transgender men and 7% non-transgender women, it is therefore striking how overrepresented trans women were within homicide statistics (NCAVP 2012). Reasons for this increased vulnerability of trans women to severe transphobic violence may relate to this population being more at risk of coming into contact with violent offenders when engaged in sex work; the finding that 18% of transphobic homicides were linked to sex work supports this (NCAVP 2012). Nemoto et al. (2004) in their study of MTF sex workers, participants stated that they were constantly at risk of 'discovery' from potential clients who did not understand their transgender identity. One participant stated that 'No one's going to kill a gay man if he finds a penis between his legs. No one's gonna kill a gay woman if he finds a pussy. But, they will definitely put a knife through a tranny's throat if they see breasts and a dick' (p. 729). Also, the sexual violence perpetrated may be used to forcefully reaffirm the victim's natal gender identity as determined by their biological sex characteristics.

Bettcher (2007) also discusses the complexity of visibility, stealth, and 'passing' in a Western heteronormative society and how these affect trans people disparately. She highlights the aforementioned 'identity enforcement' through her discussion of the Brandon Teena case where he was subjected to forced genital exposure and raped the week before his murder. Furthermore, she also considers the constant strain felt by trans people who are continually negotiating their visibility and likelihood of 'discovery' if living in stealth, realising their authentic gender identity or their inability to achieve such an authentic lifestyle. This strain may only be alleviated by continually disclosing their transgender identity. Thus, this dissonance between their authentic gender identity and the biological signifiers of gender identity as determined by Western society enables in some territories the use of the 'trans panic' defence. The fact that this defence continues to exist exacerbates the challenges already faced by trans people in society trying to achieve or maintain an authentic lifestyle. In addition, Bettcher (2007) also stated that '…it constitutes considerable emotional violence against trans people through its impeachment of moral integrity and denials of authenticity' (p. 47). Finally, to return to the point made that trans women appear to be overrepresented in transphobic hate crime statistics compared to trans men, and the high level of underreporting may be a legacy of females' lack of confidence in the criminal justice system based on previous negative experiences of institutional responses within a society based on a gendered hierarchy. In addition, the influence of masculinity and femininity, respectively, experienced by trans people prior to transitioning may influence their conceptualisation of the 'nature and meaning of violence' which may negatively affect their likelihood of reporting such crimes to the police or relevant organisations (see Moran and Sharp 2004).

Survivor Age

People under 30 years of age were more than twice as likely to experience hate-motivated physical and sexual violence, respectively (NCAVP 2012). The age of survivors can also impact on the trauma of transphobic victimisation with 41% of respondents experiencing suicidal ideation and attempting suicide, this further increased with other factors such as they were harassed/bullied in school (51%), had lost their job (55%), had low household income, or were the victim of physical assault (61%) or sexual assault (64%) (Grant et al. 2011).

Relationship with the Police

Reback et al. (2001) stated that 37% of participants were abused by the police. It should be noted that variations across statistics may be the result of sample limitations and recruitment strategies. Weisburd et al. (2000)

conducted research on a national basis on police attitudes, it was found that the reporting of police misconduct, such as the physical abuse of a suspect, 80% would not follow the 'code of silence', a quarter stated whistle-blowing was not 'worth it' and two-thirds stated they would not report because of getting the 'cold-shoulder' from colleagues. Thus, it appears that there is cognitive dissonance experienced between police officers' expressed attitudes and their behaviour. It is also noteworthy that ethnicity increased the likelihood of physical abuse and decreased the likelihood of being treated well. As Weisburd et al.'s (2000) study also suggested that 17% of officers surveyed stated that White people were treated better than Black people and other ethnic minorities and that 11% of respondents suggested that police violence against Black people is more prevalent than against White people. However, there was not a breakdown of the ethnicity of officers who provided these responses.

In addition, it was suggested that there was almost an even split that there was an increased likelihood of being arrested if the suspect expressed 'bad attitude' with 49% of officers agreeing and 51% disagreeing on this issue. Finally, it was stated that there was a strong disagreement between the attitudes of White and Black and other ethnic minority officers on the influence of ethnicity (see Weisburd et al. 2000). Although Weisburd et al.'s study was not specifically about trans people, the results may be applied to demonstrate the impact of intersectional characteristics in relation to the already negative attributions being made with regard to suspects from Black and minority ethnic backgrounds. Therefore, the influence of trans people's deviation from gender binary norms in addition to their ethnicity may further increase their chances of receiving a less than professional police response or at the other end of the scale being subjected to police misconduct. It has also been highlighted in the National Coalition of Anti-Violence Programs (NCAVP) report published in 2009 that although the number of total incidents has decreased, the number of bias police misconduct cases involving police entrapment, police raids and unjustified arrests now represent a higher percentage of hate crime incidents than was the case in 2008. In the NCAVP (2012) report, LGBTQH people from ethnic minorities were twice as likely to experience police violence.

Wolff and Cokeley (2007) found a litany of examples of unprofessional conduct regarding the police response to bias crimes such as '…'911' operators failing to send assistance, police officers mocking the victims, officers blaming the victim…[and] police laughing at victims' accounts of the situations that occurred' (p. 13). It was also noted that even when the police officer's conduct was considered appropriate, complainants still routinely stated that they felt let down due to officers not filing a basic incident report. It was found that these basic reports often required some follow-up or formal documentation, so due to the non-recording of these crimes, complainants were denied the legitimacy of the status of being a 'victim' of a crime. There are a number of reasons why there may be some resistance by the police in recording bias element of these crimes, (i) it increases the severity of the crime, (ii) it increases the paperwork to be completed and (iii) it may have a negative impact on the city's public image (Comstock 1991).

In the Transgender Discrimination Survey, the following results were found: 22% of respondents experienced harassment by the police in their interactions and this increased to between 29% and 38% when the respondent was from a minority ethnic group. Six per cent reported physical assault by police and 2% were sexually assaulted because of their transgender or gender non-conforming identity. Twenty per cent reported a denial of equal service by police and almost half of the respondents were uncomfortable seeking policing assistance (Grant et al. 2011). This lack of confidence in law enforcement and further victimisation and re-traumatisation by police in their interactions with gender non-conforming and trans people is concerning. It therefore suggests that there is a fundamental need to address the failings of police service through awareness training and improved policies when responding to trans and non-binary individuals when reporting crimes so they are treated in an equitable manner to non-transgender members of the community. The policing response to transphobic hate crime will be discussed in more detail in Chap. 5.

This chapter has examined the victim–offender relationship in the perpetration of transphobic hate crime. It focused on the motivation of offenders and their background characteristics. The likelihood of victimisation was explored with regard to factors which increase vulnerability such as gender, ethnicity, class and age. The locations where this type of crime is perpetrated were considered and how gender identity may differentially influence the notion of safe spaces and that this may increase or decrease one's susceptibility to criminal victimisation depending on whether one identifies as a trans female or trans male. Next, the policing response is discussed with regard to barriers to reporting transphobic hate crime. Also, the evolving police response with the establishment of dedicated officers who investigate these crimes and specialist officers who support these hate crime victims will be considered.

References

Anderson, E. (2008). Being masculine is not about who you sleep with...: Heterosexual athletes contesting masculinity and the one-time rule of homosexuality. *Sex Roles, 58,* 104–115.

Anti-Defamation League (ADL). (2016). *Combating hate: Hate crimes law: ADL: Hate crimes information for law enforcement: Definition of hate crime.* Retrieved from http://www.adl.org/combating-hate/hate-crimes-law/c/hate-crimes-information-for-law-enforcement.html#.V80nIJgrLIV.

Antjoule, N. (2016). *The hate crime report: Homophobia, biphobia and transphobia in the UK.* London. Retrieved from http://www.galop.org.uk/wp-content/uploads/2016/10/The-Hate-Crime-Report-2016.pdf.

Bettcher, T. M. (2007). Evil deceivers and make-believers: On transphobic violence and the politics of illusion. *Hypatia, 22*(3), 43–65.

Comstock, G. D. (1991). *Violence against lesbians and gay men.* New York: Columbia University Press.

Darley, J. M., & Latané, B. (1968). Bystander intervention in emergencies: Diffusion of responsibility. *Journal of Personality and Social Psychology, 8*(4), 377–383.

Grant, J. M., Mottet, L. A., Tanis, J., Harrison, J., Herman, J. L., & Keisling, M. (2011). *Injustice at every turn: A report of the National Transgender Discrimination Survey.* Washington. Retrieved from http://www.transe quality.org/sites/default/files/docs/resources/NTDS_Report.pdf.

Groth, A. N. (1979). *Men who rape: The psychology of the offender.* New York: Plenum Press.

Hennen, P. (2008). *Faeries, bears, and leathermen*. Chicago: University of Chicago Press.

Hindelang, M. J., Gottfredson, M. R., & Garofalo, J. (1978). *Victims of personal crime: An empirical foundation for a theory of personal victimization*. Cambridge: Ballinger.

Iganski, P., & Levin, J. (2015). *Hate crime: A global perspective*. New York: Routledge.

Kelley, P. (2009). *Filling in the blanks: Hate crime in London*. London.

Kelley, K., & Gruenewald, J. (2015). Accomplishing masculinity through anti-lesbian, gay, bisexual, and transgender homicide: A comparative case study approach. *Men and Masculinities, 18*, 3–29.

Kemnitz, D. A. (2014). *The first step: Ending the use of gay and trans panic defenses*. Retrieved from http://www.jurist.org/hotline/2014/10/darcy-kemnitz-panic-defense.php.

Kuehnle, K., & Sullivan, A. (2001). Patterns of anti-gay violence: An analysis of incident characteristics and victim reporting. *Journal of Interpersonal Violence, 16*, 928–943.

Kuehnle, K., & Sullivan, A. (2003). Gay and lesbian victimization: Reporting factors in domestic violence and bias incidents. *Criminal Justice and Behavior, 30*, 85–96.

Lombardi, E. L., Wilchins, R. A., Priesing, D., & Malouf, D. (2001). Gender violence: Transgender experiences with violence and discrimination. *Journal of Homosexuality, 42*(1), 89–101.

McDevitt, J., Levin, J., & Bennett, S. (2002). Hate crime offenders: An expanded typology. *Journal of Social Issues, 58*(2), 303–317.

McDevitt, J., Farrell, A., Rousseau, D., & Wolff, R. (2013). Hate crimes: Characteristics of incidents, victims, and offenders. In R. C. Davis, A. J. Lurigio, & S. Herman (Eds.), *Victims of crime* (4th ed., pp. 107–132). London: Sage.

Moran, L. J., & Sharpe, A. N. (2004). Violence, identity and policing: The case of violence against transgender people. *Criminal Justice, 4*(4), 395–417.

National Coalition of Anti-Violence Programmes (NCAVP). (2012). *Hate violence against lesbian, gay, bisexual, transgender, queer, and HIV-affected communities in the United States in 2011: A Report from the National Coalition of Anti-Violence programs* (pp. 1–103). New York: New York City Gay & Lesbian Anti-Violence Project.

Nemoto, T., Operario, D., Keatley, J., & Villegas, D. (2004). Social context of HIV risk behaviours among male-to-female transgenders of colour. *AIDS Care, 16*(6), 724–735.

Pascoe, C. J. (2007). *Dude, you're a fag: Masculinity and sexuality in high school.* Berkeley: University of California Press.

Rayburn, N. R., Mendoza, M., & Davison, G. C. (2003). Bystanders' perceptions of perpetrators and victims of hate crime. *Journal of Interpersonal Violence, 18*(9), 1055–1074.

Raymond, J. (1996). The politics of transgenderism. In R. Ekins & D. King (Eds.), *Blending genders: Social aspects of cross-dressing and sex changing* (pp. 215–223). London: Routledge.

Reback, C. J., Simon, P. A., Bemis, C. C., & Gatson, B. (2001). *The Los Angeles transgender health study: Community report.* Los Angeles.

Schilt, K., & Westbrook, L. (2009). Doing gender, doing heteronormativity: Doing "gender normals", transgender people, and the social maintenance of heterosexuality. *Gender and Society, 23*(4), 440–464.

Stotzer, R. L. (2009). Violence against transgender people: A review of United States data. *Aggression and Violent Behavior, 14,* 170–179.

Stotzer, R. L. (2014). Law enforcement and criminal justice personnel interactions with transgender people in the United States: A literature review. *Agression and Violent Behavior, 19,* 263–277.

Transgender Equality Network Ireland (TENI) (2014). *STAD: Stop transphobia and discrimination report.* Ireland. Retrieved from www.teni.ie.

Weisburd, D., Greenspan, R., Hamilton, E. E., Williams, H., & Bryant, K. A. (2000). Police attitudes towards abuse from authority: Findings from a national study. In National Institute of Justice (Ed.), *National Institute of Justice: Research in brief* (pp. 1–15). National Institute of Justice.

Wolff, K. B., & Cokely, C. L. (2007). "To protect and serve?" An exploration of police conduct in relation to the gay, lesbian, bisexual, and transgender community. *Sexuality and Culture, 11,* 1–23.

Xavier, J. M., Bobbin, M., Singer, B., & Budd, E. (2005). A needs assessment of trangendered people of color living in Washington, DC. *International Journal of Transgenderism, 8*(2/3), 31–48.

Xavier, J., Honnold, J. A., & Bradford, J. (2007). *The health, health related needs, and lifecourse experiences of transgender Virginians.* Virginia: Virginia Department of Health, Division of Disease Prevention through the Centers for Disease Control and Prevention.

5

Responses to Transphobic Hate Crime

Abstract In this penultimate chapter, the response to transphobic hate crime by charities, policy-makers and criminal justice agencies, such as the police and their specialist provision of dedicated police officers will be examined. Also highlighted are the limited resources of charities and police resulting in a needs-directed approach exacerbated by the extensive underreporting of transphobic hate crime which is a cause for concern. The lack of confidence in criminal justice agencies both in England and Wales and in the USA is a key contributing factor in this regard. This issue will be examined in conjunction with the methods introduced to improve reporting practices, for example, third-party reporting. This chapter will thus inform the final chapter's recommendations on responses to transphobic hate crime.

Keywords Policy · Charities · Response · Improvements · Reporting practices

The term 'response' is taken here in its broadest sense to encompass proactive approaches such as lobbying for the recognition and protection

J. Jamel, *Transphobic Hate Crime*, Palgrave Hate Studies,
https://doi.org/10.1007/978-3-319-57879-8_5

of trans and non-binary people's rights to enjoy a lifestyle free from indirect and direct forms of harm. In addition, this term also encompasses reactive responses to reports of transphobic hate crime victimisation and institutionalised discrimination on the basis of gender identity. Nonetheless, global awareness is increasing regarding the importance of responding to institutional gender discrimination and injustice levelled at trans and non-binary people as well as their victimisation as a result of transphobic hate crime. For example, the Commissioner for Human Rights stated that '...[t]ransgender people are often afforded little protection by law enforcement officials in the event of a transphobic hate crime or incident. In many cases trans people who turn to law enforcement agencies for protection are often ridiculed, harassed or just ignored, despite the positive obligation of states under the European Convention of Human Rights to investigate these crimes and bring the perpetrator to justice' (Commissioner for Human Rights 2009, p. 37). European and international initiatives will also be discussed to learn from their best practice in responding to the phenomenon of transphobic hate crime.

The next section explores some of the key charities in England which educate and lobby for transgender rights and raise awareness of these rights, as well as provide support for victims/survivors of transphobic hate crime. Please see the Appendix for a list of their contact details.

National and International Charity and Non-Governmental Responses

Information on the responses provided by select organisations is outlined below. In addition to which a more comprehensive list with details of other organisations that also offer advocacy and support to victims of transphobic hate crime through organisational support such as the Gay London Police Monitoring Group (who are one of the key organisations at the forefront of responding to transphobic hate crime) together with other pivotal agencies in this regard are also discussed here.

Gay London Police Monitoring Group (GALOP)

This is London's Lesbian Gay Bisexual Transgender community's safety charity, the aim of which is to work towards enabling the freedom of movement and safe and equitable lifestyles for LGBT people. GALOP provides advice, support and advocacy to those who have experienced homophobia, transphobia, biphobia, sexual violence or domestic abuse (as they now provide services previously delivered by *Broken Rainbow*). This organisation advocates for those who experienced problems with the policing response and also assists them with any questions regarding the criminal justice system (Antjoule 2013). For further information, see below under '*LGBT Community Third Party Reporting Initiatives*' for a description of their services. Another important organisation that educates, trains and provides advocacy and support regarding issues affecting trans people is the Gender Identity and Research Society (GIRES).

Gender Identity and Research Society (GIRES)

This organisation takes a scientific approach to researching gender dysphoria. It is a volunteer-operated membership charity to provide a voice for trans and gender non-conforming people, non-binary, and non-gender individuals and their families. This organisation also educates and provides training to external agencies. They are actively engaged in policy-making decisions which affect the diverse trans and gender non-conforming communities with regard to equality and human rights particularly in relation to health care. The latter is of particular importance when one considers the lack of sensitivity and discrimination often shown by healthcare professionals which in the case of transphobic hate crime may result in their secondary victimisation, further traumatising them. They provide training for the police and other organisations. Specialist police officers also work with them to develop and maintain links with the trans community as well as raising awareness of issues affecting the rights of trans and non-binary people.

Gendered Intelligence

This organisation is a not-for-profit Community Interest Company which was established in 2008. They work mainly with the trans community and those who influence trans lives such as educators and employers. A particular specialty of theirs is the supportive service they provide for 8–25 year olds. They deliver programmes tailored to trans youth as well as support for parents and carers. In addition, Gendered Intelligence offers trans awareness training for the professional and educational sectors (e.g. schools, colleges and universities). Their mission is to facilitate the improved understanding of the diversity of gender and challenging societal barriers to the expression of trans, non-binary and gender non-conforming gender identities being recognised and valued.

The Community Alliance to Combat Hate (CATCH)

This organisation aims to provide those who have experienced hate crime victimisation to get as much help as possible while alleviating the stress often involved in this process. It does have specific geographic catchment areas which are the London boroughs of Hackney and Westminster. However, it is stated that if you are from outside of those boroughs you can still contact them. The facilities they provide include (i) providing a safe space to talk; (ii) advising you on your rights and using them; (iii) supporting you through the reporting process if you wish to report the incident(s) to the police; (iv) guidance on financial compensation; (v) referral to other services such as counselling or accommodation; and (vi) providing practical support to help you feel safe.

It has also been highlighted in Chap. 3 when discussing legislation that in many parts of the world people in same-sex relationships and/or those who are gender-variant individuals are either ostracised or subjected to extreme punishments and even death. Thus within the constraints of this text, a snapshot of some of the key advocates and support organisations are discussed in addition to select European and International policy-making bodies to provide the reader with a sense of the varied initiatives that are all trying to tackle the heinous crime that is transphobic hate crime. The examination of these agencies and organisations begins with an American perspective and then broadens out to a more International and European perspective.

Stonewall

This organisation is a charity whose services were primarily directed at Lesbian, Gay or Bisexual people until 2015 when they broadened their remit to include trans people. Their main aim is to lobby for equality with regard to legal rights but also socially to fight against discrimination against these groups. They offer advocacy and support in relation to a number of issues which include hate crime, useful resources regarding the latter may be located on their website (see the Appendix for details). In 2017 the Stonewall Trans Advisory Group (STAG) have launched a five year plan to create equality for trans people in Britain.

USA

The following American organisations engage in a range of support, activism and advocacy are included here in order to demonstrate the variety of responses available where sex and gender-diverse people are recognised and accepted within society, certain states mentioned earlier in the text notwithstanding.

Anti-Violence Project (AVP)

The Anti-Violence Project (AVP) organisation was founded in 1980 in Chelsea, New York, in response to homophobic violence and to provide support for the gay community. Currently, it provides numerous services including the provision of free and confidential assistance to lesbian, gay, bisexual, transgender, queer and people living with HIV across the five boroughs of New York City, this translates into client services, the organising of community activism and engagement as well as public advocacy. The AVP organisation highlights the variety and extremities of transphobic violence in order to raise awareness of violence against this gender minority in addition to their work with other sexual minorities and on intimate partner violence which transgresses across all gender and sexual communities.

National Coalition of Anti-Violence Projects (NCAVP)

This organisation's aim is to take an anti-oppression approach to ending violence against members of the LGBTQ communities. In other words, their approach to tackle sexual orientation and gender-based violence is through organisation, activism and education. They also offer counselling and advocacy. Third-party reporting is also facilitated, but they do not appear to offer to pass details on to the police and thus do not act as a referral service in this regard. Instead, the data are anonymised and used to identify trends in the data and identify the level and extent of the violence perpetrated. Thus, they maintain an independent stance with regard to the reporting of transphobic hate crime, their lack of explicit referral to the police suggests a lack of confidence in a sensitive and appropriate policing response. This is consistent with the research findings detailed later in this chapter regarding police officers responding in an insensitive manner, with a lack of professionalism and empathy to transphobic hate crime victims, or even engaging in direct victimisation.

American Civil Liberties Union (ACLU)

The ACLU has a much broader scope than the AVP and is non-partisan, fights for individual freedoms against government abuse, defends civil liberties of groups they feel whose rights are being eroded or violated, irrespective of their beliefs and opinions. Here, the focus is on their lobbying for transgender rights, challenging institutional discrimination and providing education through raising awareness of issues negatively affecting the trans community and non-binary individuals. They also challenge state laws that do not as yet recognise the rights of transgender people or provide them protection (aclu.org/about/aclu-history) (ACLU 2016). Please refer to Chap. 3 for a discussion for the number of states who do not provide legal protection for trans people against harm and discrimination. Their services are important from a proactive perspective regarding the addressing of the prevalence of transphobic hate crime by educating and tackling ignorance and also supporting victims of this type of crime.

Next, a more Eurocentric perspective is taken which highlights the more collaborative approach of organisations in Europe; however, this is not to say that all of the member organisations are equitable in their responses to the protection of transgender people's rights and protection from harm.

Europe

Transgender Europe (Transgender EU)

Transgender EU has 97 member organisations across 42 countries and engages in research, lobbies for transgender human rights and raises awareness through education. They also provide training on victims' rights and hate crime monitoring, they launched the *Trans Murder Monitoring Project* in January 2008 with Liminalis (a Journal for Sex/Gender Emancipation and Resistance), and from then to April 2016, a total of 2115 reported killings of trans people in 65 countries have been registered (http://www.transrespect.org/en/idahot-2016-tmm-update/). This statistic should be interpreted as an underrepresentation of trans victims of homicides due to potential recording errors because of the variance across countries in how they record crimes, also, the transgender identity of the victim may not always be disclosed or recognised. In addition, to address the underreporting of transphobic hate crime, TGEU works with partner organisations to record discrimination, hate speech, hate crimes and offers community-based support for victims/survivors of violence in the framework of its ProTrans project (TGEU 2013). Another larger organisation called the International Lesbian Gay Trans Intersex Association (ILGA) Europe is a legal, political and social change advocate for trans people is discussed next.

International Lesbian Gay Trans and Intersex Association (ILGA) Europe

The European Region for ILGA lobbies for political, legal and social change at European level. It is a non-governmental organisation which consists of 400 organisations from 45 European countries. It advocates for human rights and equality for LGBTI people in Europe before the European Union, the Council of Europe and the Organization for the Security and Co-operation in Europe (OSCE) across a range of areas which include hate speech and hate crime. The most recent information with regard to responses to hate crime targeting these marginalised communities. This organisation therefore takes a proactive approach to initiating change that can recognise and protect transgender rights thus educating and challenging ignorance around trans issues which can foster negative and hostile attitudes towards the trans community that may culminate in transphobic hate crime (ILGA Europe 2016). Next, the European Union's contribution to address transphobia and related hate crime is considered.

European Union

The European Union (EU) does not require its member states to recognise sexual orientation, gender identity and/or gender expression as a bias motivating factor in criminal law. However, the EU's Directive on the rights of victims recognises that the nature of bias crimes and the victim's personal characteristics, including sexual orientation, gender identity and gender expression, must be part of the presence of specific needs which require protection. Individual European Union member states' legislation varies considerably at a national level although transphobia, for example, can be an aggravating factor in sentencing crimes. Incitement is also punished in penal law within some European jurisdictions. Another European organisation that addresses transphobic hate crime but from a human rights perspective is the Organisation for Security and Co-operation in Europe (OSCE) which is discusssed below.

The Organisation for Security and Co-operation in Europe (OSCE)

The OSCE's key focus is security across European territories, it takes a political and militaristic, economic, environmental and human-orientated perspective to address security issues. There are 57 participating states which all have equal status in decision-making across a range of issues which include human rights and under which hate crimes are being addressed from examining the training of law enforcement to the prevention and response to this issue. The participating states must make decisions by consensus on a political basis; however, the actions to be taken as a result of these are not legally binding. This does raise the question as to how committed these member states are to engage in decisive action, or is it more about perception and the appearance of tackling particular issues such as hate crime. The OSCE with the Office for Democratic Institutions and Human Rights (ODIHR) compiles an annual report on hate crimes in the OSCE Region—Incidents and Responses which details all reported hate crime incidents across its region. For further information on the activities of this organisation and the awareness it raises as well as the advocacy provided, please refer to the Appendix where the website details are provided to access their reports and additional resources (OSCE 2016). Next, the Council of Europe and its approach to tackling transphobic hate crime is discussed.

The Council of Europe

The Council of Europe consists of 47 member states, 28 of which are in the European Union (Directorate of Communication 2016). The Council of Europe Committee of Ministers in 2010 adopted a recommendation of historical significance to combat discrimination on the basis of sexual orientation and gender identity. The recommendation includes firm actions to address LGBTI-phobic crime and ensure systems, and procedures are effective for data collection and provide victims' protection (The Council of Europe 2011). Thus a more holistic approach is being taken to tackle this type of crime. Finally, a more global perspective is taken by outlining the United Nations approach to tackling transphobic hate crime, see below.

United Nations

On 30 June 2016, a historic vote was taken by the United Nations Human Rights Council, whereby the resolution on the 'Protection against Violence and Discrimination based on Sexual Orientation and Gender Identity' was adopted (Human Rights Watch 2016) in order to mandate an appointment for an independent expert on the subject. This is a crucial step forward as this appointment formally recognises that a more specialised response is required to address the multiple complexities involved when tackling transphobic hate crime.

In the next section, the different modes through which people can report their own or others' victimisation to the police or to charities and organisations who support victims of transphobic hate crime are described. In addition, the importance of adhering to the requirements of the Gender Recognition Act (GRA) 2004 is also highlighted below in relation to transphobic hate crime cases that are reported to the police.

UK Reporting Practices

The police must ensure when responding to hate crime victims that they do not contravene the GRA 2004 with regard to how trans people are referred to and ensure their transgender status is not disclosed without their consent, or unnecessarily during the course of responding to their criminal victimisation. It should be noted that the GRA 2004 is being reviewed in 2017 and the Scottish Government has also said it will consult on reforming this Act by the summer of this year 'to ensure our gender recognition law is in line with international best practice' (The Scottish Government 2016, p. 77).

Next, online and social media options for reporting transphobic hate crime to the police is considered.

Reporting Online and via Social Media to the Police

True Vision

True Vision provides a website that enables access to information on education, strategies and policies, support for victims and the various options available to report crimes, e.g. via the police, Crimestoppers, and third-party reporting. Information on the prosecution of hate crimes and safety tips are also made available on this site. Contact details for organisations that can support victims of transphobic hate crimes are also provided for GALOP, The Gender Trust, Mermaids (for those 17 years and younger and their families), Press for Change (UK leading experts in Transgender Law), GIRES, IMAAN (supports LGBT Muslim people), REGARD (supports LGBTQ disabled people). Hate crime data and research can also be accessed as well as information sharing agreements (http://report-it.org.uk/home). Another mode of reporting is through dedicated applications which can be downloaded onto mobile telephones such as the *Self-Evident* app.

The Self-Evident App

This is a bespoke and freely available app that can be downloaded onto smartphones which allows people to take back control after they have been a victim of a crime. It may be downloaded from the following website: https://witnessconfident.org/self-evident-app. This app provides an alternative method for reporting transphobic hate crimes, for example, whereby victims can use this app (i) to securely store visual, i.e. photographic and video evidence; (ii) for audio evidence such as the recording of reliable statements; (iii) to corroborate the evidence recorded; and (iv) to file a crime report with the police from their smartphones. This is done by tapping 'send' on the app which will result in an email link to the victim's crime report automatically being sent to the right police team in England and Wales. Furthermore, the app also has additional features for repeat and vulnerable victims which are particularly appropriate regarding transphobic hate crime (with its high rate of repeat victimisation). The relevant police force will then contact the victim by email or telephone, it can also be checked as to when the respective crime report was accessed by logging onto http://www.JustEvidence.org. There are also two strands of police response (i) the enhanced response where these crime reports are handled at the following police forces' headquarters (Bedfordshire, Cambridgeshire, Cheshire, Cumbria, Dyfed-Powys, Essex, Gloucestershire, Gwent, Hampshire, Hertfordshire, Kent, Lancashire, Leicestershire, Merseyside, Metropolitan Police [London], Greater Manchester, Norfolk, Northumbria, North Wales, North Yorkshire, South Wales, South Yorkshire, Suffolk, Surrey, Sussex, Thames Valley [Berkshire, Buckinghamshire & Oxfordshire], Warwickshire, West Mercia [Herefordshire, Shropshire & Worcestershire] and West Yorkshire); and (ii) the basic response provided by all remaining police forces in England and Wales, whereby the crime report is automatically dispatched to the local police force and as described above victims can log onto their account at *JustEvidence* to identify which police team has been assigned to the case. In the next section, reporting practices in the USA and the UK are explored in relation to the policing response to transphobic hate crime.

The Virginia Transgender Health Initiative Survey (VTHIS) found that 70% of victims of physical violence did not report these incidents to the police (see Xavier et al. 2007). Whereas Witten (2003) found that 22% of transgender victims of physical violence had reported their victimisation to the authorities and an additional 4% said they sometimes reported the incidents to the police. Of those who reported 65% were dissatisfied with the level of service received. Factors which inhibited reporting to the police included fear of reprisal by the perpetrator (21%), fear of institutionalised gender abuse within the medical and legal systems (11%), (a lack of confidence in the authorities regarding the successful handling of their case). [It was felt that irrespective of whether they reported or not there would be no difference in the response (29%)'] and some wanted to protect the perpetrator (8%). In addition, Reback et al. (2001) also found that 39% of perpetrators were police officers, thus, who can trans victims subsequently turn to when the 'protector' is also the 'perpetrator'—how can legal recourse be achieved? Another consequence of this dynamic is that trans people's confidence is further reduced regarding the securing justice and in the effectiveness of the policing response.

There is also an interesting gender differential in reporting practices, in that, trans women may report more incidents to the police than trans men because of the latter group's prior gendered experiences as women. The type and symbolism of violence as well as the poor treatment by the police with regard to the police response to their criminal victimisation may also act as inhibitors to reporting the crime (see Moran and Sharpe 2004). Moran and Sharpe also suggest that a multifaceted approach should be used by police when carrying out activities such as risk assessment, victim support and in their development of strategies of detection and prosecution of transphobic hate crime. Furthermore, there is the additional challenge of the increased complexity of such crimes which may also incorporate homophobic, domestic, racial and ethnic violence elements used to reinforce hierarchies of religion, class and other social and gender distinctions. Thus, the reticence of trans people to report criminal victimisation to the police is clearly documented in the available research (Moran and Sharpe 2002, 2004) and has been highlighted throughout this text. Also, the fear of secondary victimisation by law enforcement personnel further serves to reinforce distrust of the police and thus increases the inhibition of members of the LGBT community from reporting such crimes (Comstock 1991; US Department of Justice as cited in Wolff and Cokelely 2007).

Hate-motivated crime is usually composed of multiple rather than singular incidents therefore the police response is even more crucial; as the way the police respond when an initial incident is reported will influence future reports. It should also be borne in mind here that the initial police response when reporting a crime may influence the reporting of future crimes, irrespective of the type of crime (Jamel et al. 2008). For example, if a complainant reported a burglary and received a less than professional response, the person may not be encouraged to report a more sensitive type of crime such as a bias crime.

The next section illustrates the underreporting issue referred to in Chap. 2 which relates most strongly to the lack of confidence in the police as according to Kelley (2009) '...a significant proportion of otherwise unreported homophobic and transphobic hate incidents are either informally "told" or more formally reported to a range of agencies and organisations across London' (p. 35). The problem with this kind of reporting is that this information may not be systematically recorded or is retained by the organisation, or there are no shared recording protocols or channels of dissemination. Therefore, there may be differing conceptions of what constitutes a 'hate crime'. One recommendation to improve reporting practices was to raise awareness through media campaigns. Also highlighted was the problem of underreporting by LGBT organisations, so further research was recommended in order to understand the complexity of the issues involved (Kelley 2009).

Moran and Sharpe (2002) suggested that there were also limits regarding transgender politics within the wider remit of identity politics which should be considered in relation to the reporting and recording of 'transphobic hate crime'. These key factors include ethnicity, gender, age and social class. Other influential elements are the masculine culture of agents of the criminal justice system, such as the police and how they interpret criminal incidents, and the recording and reporting of transphobic hate crime cases. Similarly, there should not be the automatic assumption of the phenomenon of violence against trans people being filtered through the politics of 'exceptional violence' which by default normalises other types of violence against trans individuals. This approach suggests that in order to merit the case being taken seriously and hence responded to that there may be a threshold of varying levels of violence. Whereby those crimes which fail to meet this threshold are not responded to as a result of this approach and therefore normalised. Frequently, agents of law enforcement responding to an incident either may not recognise the influence of anti-LGBT bias or are reticent to classify the incident as a bias crime. However, the victim may also not wish to pursue this course of action due to the fear and stigma which may be associated with LGBT people (Wolff and Cokely 2007). In the next section, the specialist policing response that has been developed to address the challenges and failings in tackling transphobic hate crime is presented.

The policing response being discussed here is in relation to institutional gender discrimination experienced by trans and non-binary people on reporting their criminal victimisation to their direct verbal, physical and sexual victimisation at the hands of the police (see above). Thus, frequently irrespective of training, many officers fail to realise the seriousness of anti-LGBT hate crime situations. This is often illustrated by the lengthy response time, inappropriate or '…insensitive response by officers and even abusive behaviour, when responding to a call for assistance (ACLU 1997; Bureau of Justice Assistance 1999; Anti-Violence Program of the GLCAC and National Coalition of Anti-Violence Programs 1996, 2005; Kuehnle and Sullivan 2001)' (Wolff and Cokely 2007, p. 4). Furthermore, Wolff and Cokely suggest that police responses were deemed to be 'negative' when officers were considered to be 'unprofessional', that is, did not perform their routine duties, or engaged in behaviours which could be considered misconduct and/or criminal. These issues were exacerbated when officers were not sympathetic to the complainant or were reluctant in recording the incident as a bias or hate crime (Comstock 1991; Berrill and Herek 1992; Kuehnle and Sullivan 2001, 2003). There is still much improvement required with regard to the training of police and other agents within the criminal justice system and their responses to and recording of transphobic hate crime (see the Human Rights Campaign [HRC] & Trans People of Color Coalition [TPCC], 2015 for recommendations). The professional conduct expected from police officers included their being helpful, polite, '…treating victims and their situations seriously, and maintaining a professional demeanour' (Wolff and Cokely 2007, p. 16). It should be noted that the majority of the research cited above regarding the poor and sometimes even hostile policing response refers to the USA.

Nonetheless, in the UK, particularly in England and Wales, police may not have been hostile but were still failing in their efforts to provide an equitable response to LGBT victims of hate crimes compared to racial and religious bias hate crimes. Therefore, to address criticisms regarding the poor response by police to hate crimes based on victims' gender identities and sexual orientation, select police officers were encouraged to take on the more specialised role of LGBT Liaison Officer in addition to their routine first response policing duties. The role of these specialist officers is described below.

Specialist Policing Response

The key incident which initiated an improved response by the Metropolitan Police Service (MPS) in dealing with the LGB (initially later LGBT) community was the bombing of the Admiral Duncan Pub in Soho, London in 1999. The MPS is considered to be at the forefront of the specialist policing response to gender and sexual orientation-based hate crimes, but other forces also lay claim to this achievement. Tilley's (2011) conceptualisation of a problem-oriented policing model can be applied to the evolution of LGBT LOs who take a proactive rather than reactive approach. By actively engaging with the transgender community in this context, they can develop links as sources for support so that hate crimes can be reported. In addition, trends in this crime can be identified such as patterns of repeat victimisation as identified by Tilley (2003). Also, Tilley and Laycock (2002) state that 'hot classes of victim' which can relate to intersectional vulnerabilities of crime victims such as ethnicity, class and gender which are even more evident with regard to trans individuals' experiences of transphobic hate crime. Primarily, LGBT LOs assist Hate Crime Specialist Officers and Investigators and can play a crucial role in homophobic and transphobic hate crime investigations. Other responsibilities that LGBT LOs have are (i) to assist and advise units such as Community Safety Units (CSUs) in both proactive and reactive (intelligence-led) operations that involve or impact upon LGBT individuals; (ii) to act as a conduit between Hate Crime Investigators, victims and witnesses (who identify as LGBT) and provide to referrals to relevant support organisations; (iii) develop links with local LGBT groups and venues within the borough; (iv) to assist in the establishment of LGBT forums; (v) give advice, guidance and information to agencies both internal and external; and (vi) to promote and enable LGBT representations on borough IAG (Independent Advisory Groups) and Consultative Groups (MPS, n.d.). LGBT LOs' contribution to clearance and detection rates suggests there is an inherent complexity whereby the more effective the LGBT LOs are working with the trans community the higher the reporting rates will be, and these may also increase recorded crimes. Therefore, there is a potentially negative effect on performance indicators as recorded crimes should be decreasing (so this needs to be taken into account when interpreting such statistics). Thus, there may be an inverse relationship regarding the LGBT LOs' rapport with this community and their effectiveness as illustrated by recorded crime statistics. LGBT LOs are requested as specialists to advise the Hate Crime Specialist Officers who are attached to CSUs in each borough and aim to respond within a 24- to 48-hour period to reported criminal incidents. These officers are specially trained in taking video evidence to facilitate evidence being provided by vulnerable victims in accordance with Achieving Best Evidence. They also maintain contact over the telephone through welfare calls and updates on their case. In addition, they work collaboratively with community-based organisations such as GALOP discussed below and Stonewall thus providing a holistic response to transphobic hate crime.

A key role is also played by frontline officers such as first responders and the officers who staff the front desks at police stations who are crucial in the initial decision-making process of defining the crime being reported as a transphobic hate crime. Thus, these officers will assess the case criteria and decide whether to flag this as a transphobic hate crime or not. There are also protocols which must be adhered to with regard to how the complainant is addressed, and this is based on their presentation and mode of deportment, etc. However, if there is any ambiguity, and their appearance or name does not indicate gender identity, then they will be asked how they wish to be addressed. Policing resources are increasingly limited and this has resulted in their engagement in more multi-agency approaches to enable increased reporting of such crimes through third-party reporting systems. This increasing reliance on community initiatives that focus on crime prevention and problem-solving takes a more proactive approach than the traditional reactive approach to tackling crime and conflict (Engel and Worden 2003). This paradigmatic shift in the police response to crime is now even more pronounced considering the projected budget cuts across the police forces in England and Wales (Millie 2014). There are also a number of additional factors which influence the police response to criminal behaviour such as their training, attitudes, department regulations, police culture and their working environment (Kane 2002; Paoline et al. 2000; Terrill et al.

2003). Organisational priorities are also based on budgetary constraints and the need for public reassurance (see Millie 2014). Wolff and Cokely (2007) found that 76% (260) of the 342 cases required police assistance based on the reports given by callers. The police therefore have a symbiotic relationship with the AVP through offering education and outreach to officers (there are parallels here with the Metropolitan Police Service and their links with GALOP).

Recording Practices

The recording of transphobic hate crimes is not equitable with other hate crimes. For example, in a report on hate crime in the UK in 2016 (Antjoule 2016), it was stated that when an individual is found guilty of a transphobic hate crime, the motivational or hate element is not usually recorded on an individual's criminal record. The reason for this is that hate crime offences are not differentiated and identified on the Police National Computer records. The impact that this absence of detail has is that at future trials, the probation services are unaware if someone is a serial hate crime offender. This is problematic in that appropriate risk assessment work is not conducted. There is also an inconsistency between the treatment of different hate crimes, for example, specific race or faith-related offences may be recorded in a manner that highlights their hate motive which contrasts with how transphobic hate crimes are recorded as aforementioned (Antjoule 2016). This discrepancy again emphasises institutional gender discrimination in this regard. Next, the conviction rates and incongruent sentencing disposals for hate crimes are discussed.

Judicial Responses

In 2014–2015, 56 transphobic cases were referred to the Crown Prosecution Service (CPS) for a charging decision. The following year this figure increased to 98. In relation to completed prosecutions flagged as transphobic crimes on the CPS digital case management system, there were 37 in 2014–2015. This figure increased to 85 in 2015–2016. Whereas the conviction rates for transphobic hate crime cases annually were 76% (28 successful outcomes) and 80% (68 successful outcomes). It should be noted that guilty pleas were entered in 73% of successful prosecutions in 2014/2015 and 68% in the following year (CPS 2016). There is also a noteworthy inconsistency between the sentencing tariffs for different types of hate crimes. For example, there is a lower maximum sentence for transphobic than race and faith crimes in England and Wales. The following illustrates a discriminatory sentencing tariff whereby racially or religiously aggravated common assault can be given up to 2-year sentence, whereas disconcertingly for the same crime which is motivated by transphobia, the maximum is 6 months. However, Scotland has less of a discrepancy in its sentencing tariffs for hate crimes whereby a conviction for racial harassment carries a maximum sentence of seven years, whereas transphobic-motivated harassment has a maximum sentencing tariff of 5 years (Antjoule 2016). Thus, there are still significant improvements to be made to address such sentencing discrepancies in order to make the sentencing of all hate crimes equitable. Furthermore, the impact of having such discrepant sentencing tariffs is that it sends an unequivocal message to victims of transphobic hate crimes that there is a hierarchy of victimhood. Therefore, those who are victims of racial or religiously aggravated offences are considered more traumatised by their victimisation and hence these crimes attract a more severe sentence. In comparison, victims of transphobic hate crimes are thus positioned at the lower end of this hierarchy and their legitimacy as victims is undermined by the less punitive sentences assigned to such crimes. In England, particularly where the discrepancy in sentencing is quite pronounced as outlined above, it could be suggested that the sentence of six months defines these offences as minor transgressions. Next, alternatives to the incarceration of hate crime offenders are considered.

Alternatives to Imprisonment

The overcrowding in prisons and continuing budget cuts are consistently undermining the effectiveness of any possible rehabilitation while incarcerated (Prison Reform Trust 2016). It is therefore suggested that increased efforts should be made to identify alternatives to imprisonment, this would be particularly appropriate for hate crime offenders. Antjoule (2016) suggests that penalties target and challenge the underlying bias or motivation which is driving the offender's actions while simultaneously implementing specialist hate crime restorative justice programmes where applicable. Nevertheless, in the current austere climate it is recognised that the investment involved may be prohibited even though it is less than that incurred by incarcerating these offenders. Nonetheless, it should not be seen as a cost cutting exercise, instead the costs may cancel each other out due to the diversion of funds from long sentences which are expensive and instead establishing evidenced-based hate crime restorative justice and offender programmes. Thus, the aim of these programmes would be to encourage offenders to be accountable and address the biases and negative perceptions that motivate these individuals' offending behaviour (Antjoule 2016). In the next section, alternatives to reporting hate crimes to the police are explored, the emphasis being on third-party reporting systems.

LGBT Community Third-Party Reporting Initiatives

Kelley (2009) found that one in ten victims felt that the police response to the homophobic/transphobic incident was negative or unhelpful. A large percentage of victims were dissatisfied with the police response and subsequently chose to contact LGBT organisations for support and advice. Thus, the initial policing response can negatively affect reporting practices, so further attention should be given to improving the police response in this regard. GALOP in their assisted reporting role provides detailed information about transphobic incidents, by taking case notes, recording demographic details and information about the nature of the incident. It was also found that '[t]rans people were twice as likely to contact LGBT organisations about verbal abuse or threats compared to non-trans people. Trans people were [also] more likely to contact LGBT organisations about repeated harassment. Nearly, three-quarters of trans victims experienced repeated transphobic/homophobic harassment compared to over half of non-trans victims' (Kelley 2009, p. 53). Furthermore, Kelley states that the result of these reporting practices was that 37% of respondents reported to the police versus 46% who reported to LGBT organisations. Thus, demonstrating a reluctance to contact the police and the decreasing level of confidence in them which continues to be a problem when the low-reporting rates are examined, and even more so when the detection rates in London are considered. For example only 6% of 51 cases were recorded as being detected for the period of 2012/2013, this was the lowest figure since these crimes were recorded (Antjoule 2013). Thus, demonstrating that more still needs to be done by the police in order to increase the confidence of the gay and trans communities in the professionalism and sensitivity of their police service response.

Kelley (2009) therefore found that the limitations of the police response to transphobic hate crime were regarding the accessibility and quality of services from the Community Safety Units (CSUs) and Lesbian Gay Bisexual Transgender Liaison Officers (LGBT LOs). For example, it was found that it was difficult to get through to CSUs and LGBT LOs on the telephone as (i) "[c]alls were not answered or went directly to answer machine and a response was given only after a number of days" and (ii) contact details were incorrect or "out of date on websites" (Kelley 2009, p. 33). There was also a lack of consistency with regard to the promotion of LGBT LOs within the LGBT community, with some officers being more proactive than others in raising awareness of their role. Furthermore, most transphobic hate crime victims were still unaware of these officers. Thus, better marketing of these officers' services and the fostering of links with the LGBT community are required. In the main, LGBT LOs are part-time and are balancing their routine first response duties with these more specialised responsibilities resulting in occupational strain which may result in a less than optimal service due to resource constraints. Thus, it appears there are parallels here with the challenges faced by traditional chaperone officers who worked sex crime cases, balancing this role with their routine police duties, this role conflict was later eased with the evolution of dedicated officers such as Sexual Offences Investigative Technique (SOIT) officers and more recently Specially Trained Officers (STOs) (see Jamel et al. 2008). The MPS and LGBT LOs involvement with local third-party reporting initiatives also lacked consistency (Kelley 2009); this issue was not addressed in Antjoule (2016) as to whether the situation had improved or not, but may be followed up in future reports.

This chapter briefly discussed the importance of the GRA 2004 in England and Wales with regard to the sensitivities around disclosure of an individual's gender identity in the context of transphobic hate crime victimisation and the handling of such cases by the police. However, the key focus of the chapter was the responses to transphobic hate crime in the widest sense, from proactive approaches by specialist LGBT LOs, charity and non-governmental organisations regarding the raising awareness of issues that affect trans and non-binary people, to the traditional reactive police response to the reporting of transphobic hate crime. In addition to which the American and European contexts were discussed with regard to International organisational responses challenging the violation of trans people's rights and freedom to live a life free from fear and harassment irrespective of their gender identity. In Chap. 6, recommendations are suggested based on the above considerations as to how transphobic hate crime can be more effectively addressed.

References

ACLU. (2016). *ACLU history: Some highlights: Why we do what we do: How we do it.* Retrieved from http://www.aclu.org/about/aclu-history.

Antjoule, N. (2013). *The hate crime report: Homophobia, biphobia and transphobia in London.* London: GALOP.

Antjoule, N. (2016). *The hate crime report: Homophobia, biphobia and transphobia in the UK*. London. Retrieved from http://www.galop.org.uk/wp-content/uploads/2016/10/The-Hate-Crime-Report-2016.pdf.

Berrill, K. T., & Herek, G. M. (1992). Primary and secondary victimization in anti-gay hate cirmes: Official response and public policy. In G. M. Herek & K. T. Berrill (Eds.), *Hate crimes: Confronting violence against lesbians and gay men* (pp. 289–305). Newbury Park: Sage.

Commissioner for Human Rights. (2009). *Human rights and gender identity* (pp. 1–53). Strasbourg: Office for the Commissioner of Human Rights & The Council of Europe.

Comstock, G. D. (1991). *Violence against lesbians and gay men*. New York: Columbia University Press.

CPS. (2016). *Hate crime report 2014/2015 & 2015/2016*. London: Author.

Directorate of Communication. (2016). *The Council of Europe: An overview*. Strasbourg: Council of Europe. Retrieved from https://edoc.coe.int/en/an-overview/6966-the-council-of-europe-an-overview.html.

Engel, R. S., & Worden, R. E. (2003). Police officers' attitudes, behavior, and supervisory influences an analysis of problem-solving. *Criminology, 41*(1), 131–166.

Gender Recognition Act (GRA) (2004). Retrieved from http://www.legislation.gov.uk/ukpga/2004/7/contents.

Human Rights Campaign & Trans People of Color Coalition. (2015). *Addressing anti-transgender violence: Exploring realities, challenges and solutions for policy-makers and community advocates*. Retrieved from http://hrc-assets.s3-website-us-east-1.amazonaws.com//files/assets/resources/HRC-AntiTransgenderViolence-0519.pdf.

Human Rights Watch. (2016). *UN makes history on sexual orientation, gender identity: Human Rights Body establishes an independent expert*. Retrieved from https://www.hrw.org/news/2016/06/30/un-makes-history-sexual-orientation-gender-identity.

ILGA Europe. (2016). *Our advocacy work: Hate crime and hate speech*. Retrieved from http://www.ilga-europe.org/what-we-do/our-advocacy-work/hate-crime-hate-speech.

Jamel, J., Bull, R., & Sheridan, L. (2008). An investigation of the police service provided to male rape survivors. *International Journal of Police Science and Management, 10*, 486–508.

Kane, R. J. (2002). The social ecology of police misconduct. *Criminology, 40*(4), 867–896.

Kelley, P. (2009). *Filling in the blanks: Hate crime in London*. London: GALOP.

Kuehnle, K., & Sullivan, A. (2001). Patterns of anti-gay violence: An analysis of incident characteristics and victim reporting. *Journal of Interpersonal Violence, 16,* 928–943.

Kuehnle, K., & Sullivan, A. (2003). Gay and lesbian victimization: Reporting factors in domestic violence and bias incidents. *Criminal Justice and Behavior, 30,* 85–96.

Metropolitan Police Service (MPS). (1995). Lesbian Gay Bisexual Transgender Liaison Officer [LGBT LO] job description & role profile (p. 1). London: Author.

Millie, A. (2014). What are the police for? Re-thinking policing post-austerity. In J. M. Brown (Ed.), *The future of policing* (pp. 1–11). Abingdon: Routledge.

Moran, L. J., & Sharpe, A. N. (2002). Policing the transgender/violence relation. *Current Issues in Criminal Justice, 13*(3), 269–285.

Moran, L. J., & Sharpe, A. N. (2004). Violence, identity and policing: The case of violence against transgender people. *Criminal Justice, 4*(4), 395–417.

OSCE. (2016). *Who we are.* Retrieved from http://www.osce.org/whatistheosce.

Paoline, E. A., Myers, S., & Worden, R. E. (2000). Police culture, individualism, and community policing: Evidence from two police departments. *Justice Quarterly, 17*(3), 575–605.

Prison Reform Trust. (2016). *Prison: The facts: Bromley briefings summer 2016* (pp. 1–12). London: Author.

Reback, C. J., Simon, P. A., Bemis, C. C., & Gatson, B. (2001). *The Los Angeles transgender health study: Community report.* Los Angeles.

Terrill, W., Paoline, E. A., & Manning, P. K. (2003). Police culture and coercion. *Criminology, 41,* 1003–1034.

TGEU. (2013). TGEU eNews. Online. Retrieved from http://tgeu.org/tgeu-newsletter-issue-3-2013/.

The Council of Europe. (2011). *Combating discrimination on grounds of sexual orientation or gender identity: Council of Europe Standards.* Strasbourg: Author.

The Scottish Government. (2016). *A plan for Scotland: The government's programme for Scotland 2016–17.* Edinburgh: Author.

Tilley, N. (2003). Community policing, problem-oriented policing and intelligence-led policing. In T. Newburn (Ed.), *Handbook of policing* (pp. 311–339). Cullompton: Willan.

Tilley, N. (2011). Modern approaches to policing: Community, problem-oriented and intelligence led. In T. Newburn (Ed.), *Handbook of policing* (2nd ed., pp. 373–403). Abingdon: Taylor & Francis.

Tilley, N., & Laycock, G. (2002). *Working out what to do: Evidence-based crime reduction* (Crime Reduction Series Paper 11). London: Home Office.

Witten, T. M. (2003). Life-course analysis—The courage to search for something more: Middle adulthood issues in the transgender and intersex community. *Journal of Human Behavior in the Social Environment, 8*(2/3), 189–224.

Wolff, K. B., & Cokely, C. L. (2007). "To protect and serve?" An exploration of police conduct in relation to the gay, lesbian, bisexual, and transgender community. *Sexuality and Culture, 11,* 1–23.

Xavier, J., Honnold, J. A., & Bradford, J. (2007). *The health, health related needs, and lifecourse experiences of transgender Virginians.* Virginia: Virginia Department of Health, Division of Disease Prevention through the Centers for Disease Control and Prevention.

6
Conclusions and Recommendations

Abstract The aim of this unique book is to raise awareness of the phenomenon of transphobic hate crime and examine its multifaceted nature. The diversity of trans people within indigenous cultures, national and international societies and their experiences of this crime are considered at the outset, as these groups are often overlooked in the Western-centric literature on transphobic hate crime. Indigenous communities' accommodation of 'third gender' identities vary in their success but are more inclusive of trans people in their respective cultures. This perspective challenges the popular notion of the homogenous trans person and emphasises the importance of addressing hate crime which can affect trans people in their daily lifestyle. It can vary in its severity and impact on the individual and their community. The victim–offender relationship and offender motivations are also examined together with the responses to this crime as well as the provision of support and advocacy available for survivors. Thus, this text provides a holistic perspective on this under-researched crime and underserved trans communities.

Keywords Awareness · Recommendations · Conclusions
Impetus for research · Reporting practices

J. Jamel, *Transphobic Hate Crime*, Palgrave Hate Studies,
https://doi.org/10.1007/978-3-319-57879-8_6

This text aims to raise awareness of the phenomenon of transphobic hate crime and the diversity of trans people within indigenous cultures and more commercialised national and international societies and their experiences of this crime. The homogeneity of trans people and the transgender community is questioned through the discussion of indigeneous trans people and their communities and cultures; in addition to their daily experiences of direct and indirect transphobic victimisation. All of which are described in Chap. 1. The gender flexibility subscribed to by many of cultures provides more scope for the expression of a multiplicity of gender presentations such as in some of the First Nation Native American tribes. Nevertheless, there are limits of acceptance whereby transphobic verbal, sexual and physical violence may be condoned (e.g. see the sections on the *alyha*, *hijra*, and *travesti*). Furthermore, as with all types of hate crime they are often rooted more in fear of difference than individualised hate, as the target person may not even be acquainted with or have had a prior relationship with the perpetrator. Instead, the hate crime incident may be levelled at the trans or non-binary person in order to send a symbolic message to the rest of the community.

Next, the key points of the chapters are explored to remind the reader that transphobic hate crime can range from a passing negative comment about the person's inability to authenticate an appearance aligned with their gender identity which may be experienced on a daily basis to more extreme violence which can result in the victim's death. It should also be noted that there has been some criticism of the available literature on transphobic hate crime regarding the tendency to focus on sexual or more extreme physical violence which exceptionalises this type of transphobic hate crime and by virtue of this renders more everyday forms of harassment abuse such as verbal violence such as slurs and derogatory name calling invisible or even normalised. The reason being that due to the frequency and consequently the resilience developed by those targeted trans individuals they do not self-identify as victims, and hence do not conceptualise this type of behaviour as criminal and the perpetration of a sexual orientation and/or gender identity-based hate crime.

Furthermore, it was also important within this text to highlight the disproportionality of research on this topic, the focus being on the experiences of White trans people which may be due to sample biases and reluctance of trans people from other ethnic backgrounds to engage with research. Nevertheless, trans people of all ethnicities deserve to have their voices heard regarding their victimisation experiences and in order to also address what support is required and their service needs. It is therefore emphasised that further research is required that takes a more intersectional approach examining the differential experiences of trans people based on their gender, ethnicity, socio-economic status and geographical location. Moreover, transphobic hate crime is not uppermost in the social consciousness compared with other types of hate crime, such as racial or religious hate crimes. This may be due to a number of reasons explored throughout this book and synopsised below under the individual chapters.

In the Introduction, a comprehensive overview of the subject of transphobic hate crime with regard to how it is defined is provided. In Chap. 1, a broader view of transgender people across indigenous cultures highlighting similarities and differences with regard to their treatment by non-transgendered traditional communities and their experiences of transphobic violence is provided. Chapter 2 discusses hate crime prevalence nationally in England and internationally in Europe and the USA. It is important to not underestimate the prevalence and impact of transphobic hate crime on an already marginalised and underserved gender community despite the low incidence in reported and recorded official statistics. Chapter 3 critically considers the legal protection of trans people regarding their rights to a lifestyle free from harassment and from infringement of their civil liberties. This is examined by discussing England and Wales, Scotland and Northern Ireland as well as Ireland; other European Countries where information was available and also the USA. The key focus of this chapter was an Anglo-American perspective due to the availability of information on the legal situation relating to the treatment of transphobic hate crime under the law in these territories.

Chapter 4 examined the victim–offender relationship paying particular attention to the impact of primary and secondary victimisation together with an examination of who the perpetrators are. Also, discussed here is the reticence to enforce the legal rights of trans and non-binary people enabling them to be active citizens and not have to negotiate gender safe spaces due to people's lack of understanding and fear of difference. The latter is inherent in all types of hate crime but appears to be more extreme with regard to gender identity- and sexual orientation-based hate crimes due to perpetrators' fear that these non-heteronormative identities and orientations threaten their respective core heterosexual and gender binary identities. Those who perpetrate these crimes are predominantly male and it is therefore suggested that they are striving towards an idealised masculinity or maleness which has parallels with Connell's (1987) conceptualisation of hegemonic masculinity. This form of masculinity is aspirational and stereotypes males as unemotional, stoic, macho, revering masculine qualities and rejecting any feminine characteristics such as passivity, sensitivity and being emotional. Thus, transphobic hate crime offenders perceive gender flexibility as undermining hegemonic masculinity. Chapter 5 examines how the crime is responded to by the police, charities and non-governmental organisations. This chapter explored how effective the response of the police is regarding transphobic hate crime, and specialist officers' and their role in engendering confidence in the trans community in order to help facilitate increased reporting of such crimes. In conjunction with this, the many other facilities that are available to transgender victims of hate crimes are considered, as community organisations also provide services (some being more specialised than others, e.g. GALOP). These organisations are becoming increasingly important considering police budget cuts which are consistent feature of this landscape and affecting the level of service they can provide. This issue is underscored by the fact that as might be expected in this economic climate that services are needs-directed, and if this need is not evidenced by reporting rates then services are negatively affected. This is particularly an issue when one considers the low level of reporting with regard to transphobic hate crime.

It is therefore suggested that there is a fundamental need to address the documented failings of the police service through more comprehensive trans awareness training and improved policies when responding to trans and non-binary individuals when reporting crimes so they are treated in an equitable manner to non-transgender members of the community.

While it is noteworthy that many of the police forces in England, for example, have specialist officers who respond to transphobic hate crimes as part of the diversity of hate crimes being responded to. The Lesbian Gay Bisexual and Transgender Liaison Officers (LGBT LOs) of the Metropolitan Police Service are the most established and have the largest number of officers, who also advise Hate Crime Specialist Officers. Nonetheless, resource and budgetary constraints can impact on training provisions and prioritisation of duties, particularly with regard to officers working part-time in this role, which can significantly impact on the quality of service delivery. The problem of low-reporting is compounded by the lack of confidence in the police nationally and internationally to effectively respond to transphobic hate crime which is exacerbated when as documented in Chap. 4 the perpetrators can sometimes be police officers. Thus, overall in relation to the policing response, there are always improvements to be made in service delivery and improving the relationship between officers and trans people, these issues are being targeted by the specialist officers discussed above but this is a gradual process.

Another way in which more confidence could be engendered in the policing response to transphobic hate crime could be the increased recruitment of trans people within the police service. This would demonstrate that attitudes are actively changing within the police to gender and sexual diversity. Although, tempering this suggestion are (i) historically the positive recruitment of officers of ethnic minority members was attempted and this was unsuccessful due to the pervasive fear of discrimination within the police service; and (ii) potential recruits would have to disclose their transgender status which is problematic. In the next section, a number of recommendations are outlined to assist in tackling transphobic hate crime.

Recommendations

Based on the issues discussed throughout this text and those particularly highlighted in the previous chapter, as well as drawing on suggestions made in a recent report by Antjoule (2016), the following recommendations are suggested. First, there needs to be more clarity with regard to the criteria for the recording of transphobic hate crimes, as was noted earlier in the text the transphobic element of certain crimes may not always be recorded. Also, the current practice may distort official statistics recorded by the police in relation to this type of crime. Second, the referral processes by police need to be reviewed so that specialist services are referred to, in addition to more generalist services like Victim Support. Third, as identified in Chap. 3, there is a lot of progress to be made with regard to legislative changes to protect trans people from transphobic hate crime. Examples include expanding Northern Irish hate crime laws to also target transphobic hate crime, passing the proposed Criminal Law (Hate Crime) Amendment Bill in Ireland, and in Europe targeting the deficiencies in law in countries such as Bulgaria, the Czech Republic, Germany, Italy and Latvia. Furthermore, it is recommended that the remaining states in the USA who have insufficient state legislation to target transphobic hate crime and address these deficits. These changes in legislation at a national and international level would enable transgender people to travel more freely and would assist in mitigating their concerns for their personal safety. Nevertheless, it should be emphasised that changing legislation is just the beginning as while this is progress, attitude change takes much longer to take effect in relation to the social acceptance of trans people.

Fourth, the hate motivation of the offender's conviction regarding transphobic hate crimes should be noted on their record to enable criminal justice authorities to identify serial offenders and address their offending behaviour in a more targeted manner, such as through educational programmes. Furthermore, due to the overburdened penal system which is suffering from budget cuts, staffing shortages and overcrowding, alternatives to incarceration should be more seriously considered, such as the increased use of restorative justice where appropriate for these offenders, and the development of guidance on best practice in this regard.

Fifth, in England the entitlement of victims' rights under the Victims Code should be given a legal basis to ensure they are enforceable. Sixth, it is recommended to professionalise and increase support and advocacy work regarding the prevention of transphobic hate crime both off-line and online through community-based initiatives. Sixth, the development of a regular survey of LGBT perceptions of hate crime affecting members of these communities should be actioned in order to compare it with changes in officially recorded hate crime. In addition, the 'T' (Transgender) element of this survey should be more inclusive and not merely tokenistic.

Educational institutions such as schools and universities should also provide a more inclusive curriculum recognising more fluid gender identities. This is in order to assist in loosening the bindings of the socially constructed rigid gender dyad which inherently places pressure on both women and men to adhere to idealised forms of masculinity and femininity which can further problematize the transitioning process for trans women in particular. This embeddedness of the binary male/female gender role which is more pronounced in Western society but also present to differing extents in indigenous cultures and non-Western territories designates all other gender identities as being deviant or 'Othered' from heteronormative and heteropatriarchal societal norms. Irrespective of geography, societies need to become more accepting of trans and gender non-conforming people and less threatened by them. Institutional gender discrimination within the criminal justice system must also be attended to as transphobic hate crime deserves to be recognised and addressed on an equal footing with other hate crimes. Resources for support and advocacy for transphobic hate crime victims can be found in the Appendix.

Finally, this book has highlighted the impact of transphobic hate crime on trans people and their lifestyles and thus encourages the reader to challenge the notion of a rigid gender binary and embrace the concept of a gender flexible society.

References

Antjoule, N. (2016). *The hate crime report: Homophobia, biphobia and transphobia in the UK*. London. Retrieved from http://www.galop.org.uk/wp-content/uploads/2016/10/The-Hate-Crime-Report-2016.pdf.

Connell, R. W. (1987). *Gender and power: Society, the person and sexual politics*. Cambridge: Polity Press.

Appendix

Web Contact Details of Organisations and Agencies discussed in Chap. 5.

UK

The Community Alliance to Combat Hate (CATCH)

W: http://www.catch-hatecrime.org.uk/

Gay London Police Monitoring Group (GALOP)

W: http://www.galop.org.uk

Gender Identity and Research Society (GIRES)

W: http://www.gires.org.uk

Stonewall

W: http://www.stonewall.org.uk/search/transphobic%20hate%20crime

True Vision

W: http://www.report-it.org.uk/home

J. Jamel, *Transphobic Hate Crime*, Palgrave Hate Studies,
https://doi.org/10.1007/978-3-319-57879-8

Europe

Transgender Europe (Transgender EU)

W: http://www.tgeu.org/

International Lesbian Gay Trans and Intersex Association (ILGA) Europe

W: http://www.ilga-europe.org/

USA

Anti-Violence Project

W: http://www.avp.org/about-avp

National Coalition of Anti-Violence Projects (NCAVP)

W: http://www.avp.org/about-avp/national-coalition-of-anti-violence-programs

American Civil Liberties Union (ACLU)

W: http://www.aclu.org/

Index

J. Jamel, *Transphobic Hate Crime*, Palgrave Hate Studies,
https://doi.org/10.1007/978-3-319-57879-8

CPI Antony Rowe
Eastbourne, UK
November 26, 2019